SYRIAC MANUSCRIPTS
IN THE HARVARD COLLEGE LIBRARY
A CATALOGUE

HARVARD SEMITIC MUSEUM
HARVARD SEMITIC STUDIES

Edited by
Frank Moore Cross

Number 23

SYRIAC MANUSCRIPTS
IN THE HARVARD COLLEGE LIBRARY
A CATALOGUE
by
Moshe H. Goshen-Gottstein

Moshe H. Goshen-Gottstein

SYRIAC MANUSCRIPTS
IN THE HARVARD COLLEGE LIBRARY

A CATALOGUE

Scholars Press

Distributed by
Scholars Press
PO Box 5207
Missoula, Montana 59806

SYRIAC MANUSCRIPTS
IN THE HARVARD COLLEGE LIBRARY
Collections from the Harvard Semitic Museum
and the
American Board of Commissioners for Foreign Missions
A CATALOGUE
with Appendices on Syriac Collections
in the Libraries of the Harvard Divinity School
and the
Union Theological Seminary, New York
by
Moshe H. Goshen-Gottstein

Library of Congress Cataloguing in Publication Data

Goshen-Gottstein, Moshe Henry, 1925-
  Syriac Manuscripts in the Harvard College
Library

  (Harvard Semitic Studies; no. 23)
  Includes index.
  1. Manuscripts,   Syriac—Massachusetts—
Cambridge—Catalogs. 2. Manuscripts, Syriac—
New York (City)—Catalogs. 3. Harvard
University Library. Houghton Library.
4. Andover-Harvard Theological Library. 5. New
York (City). Union Theological Seminary. I. Title.
II. Series: Harvard Semitic series; no. 23.
Z6605.S9G67   016.091   77-13132
ISBN 0-89130-189-5

Typesetting: Academic Press, Jerusalem, Israel

Printed in the United States of America
1   2   3   4   5
Edwards Brothers, Inc.
Ann Arbor, Michigan 48104

To Frank Cross

With fond memories of a year of strengthened friendship

INTRODUCTION

I

Every introduction is, in a way, an apology. Yet for this volume I can plead no mitigating circumstances. I had no business getting involved in a description of the Harvard Syriac manuscripts in the first place. Once begun, I should have stopped. If there is such a thing as priority in one's work, every other project I was involved in was more likely to be finished first.

As the field has developed during this century, Syriac studies in the broadest sense lie outside the province of the Semitist — an endangered species, in any case. Whereas the Semitist may still possess some competence in the language, a collection such as this should have been tackled by a student of Christian origins, of *Oriens Christianus,* of liturgy and patrology. If not a latter day Wright or Sachau, then a J. Rendell Harris, Mingana, or van Lantschoot.

When I first came to Harvard in 1960 to look at Syriac manuscripts, they had been around for many decades, arousing little interest. Nobody seemed to mind very much and nobody knew any details. Like other visitors, I started studying the MSS for my own purposes, but I got stuck. The present volume is the result.

I am not sure, even at this late hour, what made me go ahead — particularly since this work meant neglecting deadlines for volumes in series for which I bear responsibility. Perhaps I underestimated the task. But, more likely, I felt this to be a challenge different from those I ordinarily meet. I had to prove to myself I could do it. Since I have been preaching for many years that "knowing" a language does not consist of one's ability to decipher a text with the help of a dictionary, and since I entertained doubts whether anyone apart from a few specialists in Christian writings still "knows" Syriac — I set out to test myself. Since my own interest in Syriac is usually limited, I had to acquire some knowledge as regards Christian writers and writings and tread some paths usually left untrodden by Jewish students of Syriac.

I am afraid that the result of my efforts to penetrate this area will appear to a Christian specialist as incompetent as his endeavors to me, had he attempted to classify texts from the Geniza or medieval Hebrew prayerbooks of different rites. I am not sure, in the end, that the fact that no better equipped scholar had come forward was an adequate excuse for the undertaking.

There may be some additional justification for my wish to bring this catalogue to some kind of conclusion. This is not the catalogue of a well defined existing collection. To a certain extent, the collection, as here described, bears the imprint of my activity, on and off for almost two decades. Having had the pleasure, time and again, to come to Harvard, I almost felt as if the collection was part of "our" responsibility — "our" referring to the Department of Near Eastern Languages and Civilizations. This gets me to my next point.

This catalogue is the result of a feeling of strong mutual loyalties — to a point where each partner felt, in the end, that he could not let the other down. The work would have never been brought to completion but for the unfailing support and loyalty of one of my dearest friends, Frank Moore Cross. Cross was at the time — and is again — director of the Semitic Museum at Harvard. The bulk of the collection belongs to the Museum, and thus falls within the field of his authority. It was only natural that, back in 1960, the idea came up that the rough notes I had taken down for myself might be used for a catalogue. That was my fatal mistake — and his. It was Cross who gently reminded me, from time to time, that the arrangement still stood and it was he who shouldered the burden of arranging for the funds. He felt obliged to fulfill his part; I had to fulfill mine.

8

II

When I first became interested in the Harvard collection as a possible source for materials for the study of the Syriac Bible[1] almost all the manuscripts of the Semitic Museum had just been transferred to the Houghton library.[2] To be sure, Houghton already had some Syriac holdings. Thus, almost by accident, quite a sizeable collection had come together.

Most travellers in search of manuscripts have experienced the disappointment on being told that they would have to go through a collection because no list was available.[3] The student is thus forced to look at all MSS, often missing what he was actually looking for.

During 1960–61, I kept searching for an earlier description of the Harvard Syriac MSS. Nothing was known, neither in the Museum nor in the library. Yet I had reason to believe that some kind of description existed. In my talks with the late Professor Harry A. Wolfson, he brought up the name of a student who prepared a thesis, back in the twenties: Lewis H. Titterton. That student was working on a catalogue of Syriac MSS as his doctoral dissertation; but nobody seemed to know what had happened to him and his work.[4] Wolfson's recollec-

---

[1] Cf. *Textus* 2 (1962) 28 f. I have delayed publications from the collection until this catalogue becomes available. The first item has just been published. Cf. "A new text from the Syrohexapla: Deuteronomy 34" in *A Tribute to Arthur Vööbus* (ed. Robert H. Fischer), Chicago 1977, 19 f.

[2] Note the official *Report of the President of Harvard College and Reports of Departments* 1959–60 on the Semitic Museum, as written by Cross.

[3] Note the repeated remarks of Vööbus about his experiences, even as regards a library such as St. Mark's in Jerusalem, where the existing handwritten list apparently was not available for some time. Unfortunately, Macomber, *ZDMG Suppl* 1 (1969) 473 is not quite correct in saying that *all* Jerusalem MSS were included in Baumstark, *Geschichte der syrischen Literatur* (1922). But cf. his lists in *Oriens Christianus* 1–3 (1911–13).

[4] The material which subsequently turned up leaves no doubt, for it is entitled: presented according to the regulations for Candidates for

9

tions were correct, for in some volumes I found slips bearing Titterton's name.

When I left in 1961, carrying with me notes for a handlist of Syriac MSS, I urged my colleagues to keep looking for Titterton's lost materials. They finally turned up in a dark corner in the cellar of the Semitic Museum in the spring of 1963. Dr. W.H. Bond — then Curator of Manuscripts and presently Librarian of Houghton — kindly forwarded a copy to me in Jerusalem.

Titterton's descriptions — which covered a considerable part of the collection as it stands now[5] — were a most welcome tool to check my own notes against. But they also prevented publication of my catalogue. There were many discrepancies, and I had to recheck the collection to resolve them.[6] This was not to be before 1969–70.

It would appear that my drawing attention to the collection (see note 1) had caused renewed interest. In any event, W.F. Macomber looked at the collection in pursuit of his studies in liturgy and made some notes, as did the scholars who worked on the Peshitta Project in Leiden. In the fall of 1962 J.T. Clemons requested some information in connection with a census of Syriac MSS in America he wished to publish.[7] There is no point dwelling on all the misstatements in his list,

the Degree of Doctor of Philosophy. When I checked in the Harvard University Archives in 1970, it turned out that they have no record of such a dissertation and of the degree having been awarded. Titterton seems to have left Harvard about 1925 — Wolfson had some recollection of him having entered the publishing industry.

[5] Titterton dealt with most of the collection of the Semitic Museum. In 1925 there was no Houghton Library, and some of the codices which came to Houghton from sources other than the Semitic Museum are included in Titterton's list.

[6] In hindsight, this was when I should have got out.

[7] J.T. Clemons, "A Checklist of Syriac Manuscripts in the United States and Canada," *Orientalia Christiana Periodica* 32 (1966) 224 f., 478 f. (offprint). See his note p. 231. It goes without saying that I encouraged Clemons not to wait for my catalogue, especially when I realized a few months later, that I could not finalize. Clemons came

10

because Clemons was only coordinating information handed to him and never studied the manuscripts themselves.

In 1970 I took some time off for rechecking my list and for preparing the pre-final draft.[8] Only upon returning to Harvard in 1976–77 was I able to finalize. But there remains little doubt that if publication were delayed till my next Sabbatical, I would find plenty to correct.

On my last two visits to Harvard I enjoyed the cheerful cooperation of Mr. Rodney G. Dennis, the present Curator of Manuscripts at Houghton[9] as well as the continued interest of Houghton's Librarian. I am grateful for their faith in spite of their conviction that no traveller will ever finish his promised catalogue. My thanks also go to the patient staff of the Houghton Reading Room.

III

Every student of Syriac hankers after the standard of excellence set by Wright's catalogue of the British Museum.[10]

back to the Harvard MSS in his *Index of Syriac MSS containing the Epistles and the Apocalypse* published in *Studies and Documents* (ed. J. Geerlings) 33 (1968). Cf. also *Orientalia Christiana Analecta* 1974: 505 f. Incidentally, in his listing of N.T. manuscripts Clemons mentions the existence of a MS from the third century. In light of MS Syr 176 of this catalogue I can only say that I would triple-check such a claim.

[8] A copy has been available at Houghton in the office of the Curator of MSS, but it was not intended for public use.

[9] In 1970, Mr. Dennis had tables of concordances between numbers prepared — this was carried out by Mr. Joseph McCarthy of the Houghton staff. Mr. Dennis himself prepared the list attached to this volume so that scholars can easily identify the new shelfmarks with earlier numberings (Harris, Clemons, etc.) and order according to the exact shelfmark. Cf. note 44. To be sure, each description in the catalogue is introduced by the known previous listings. In addition, Mr. Dennis also read a copy of this introduction and made some suggestions.

[10] When I finished my draft in 1970, I was painfully aware of the fact that Wright's catalogue had been published exactly one hundred years earlier.

That standard was never attained again, even not by Wright himself.[11] But assuming that one possesses the learning and the capability (and happens to be officially employed for that task), it would serve no purpose to try and imitate that model. The great catalogues of the 19th century not only dealt with superb collections. They also served as treasuries for sample publications of the choicest morsels and for learned discussion. A catalogue was the outcome of intimate knowledge by a specialist, who had studied every manuscript intensively.[12]

There is a more formidable problem. Scholars of Syriac in former days arranged their own files as regards parallels and whereabouts of each unit contained in a MS. There were a few known libraries, and one could easily cross-index. It was meaningful to add comparative notes, and the author of a catalogue was expected to know what was in Rome, Paris and Oxford when describing the holdings of London.

I admit that I toyed with the idea of supplying such information. After some attempts I gave up. At a rough estimate, the number of known MSS in East and West since Baumstark's *GSL* has at least doubled. The author of a catalogue may mention some items of special interest; but he

---

[11] Wright's catalogue of the British Museum is of quite a different order than his Cambridge Catalogue, written some three decades later, when Wright did not serve any more as keeper of manuscripts. To be sure, the type of description cannot be divorced from the type of collection described.

[12] This characterization may vary from scholar to scholar, but on principle it remains true for the authors of the large catalogues of the past generation, like Mingana or van Lantschoot. While Cyril Moss will remain for me personally the last librarian of *Syriaca*, van Lantschoot is the last professional keeper who worked on his large collection of manuscripts with enviable competence. But, then, only the Vatican can still boast a *scriptor orientalis*. Cf. his *Inventaire des manuscrits syriaques des fonds Vatican* (490–631)..., *Studi e Testi* 243 (1965). Note also the painstaking work of I. Assfalg in *Syrische Handschriften* (*Verzeichnis der Orientalischen Handschriften in Deutschland*, V) 1963. That type of catalogue can be expected if Vööbus manages to publish the lists of treasures he found.

cannot be expected to offer raw materials for students of comparative armchair catalogue literature.[13]

Another point is worth mentioning. Professional students of MSS will formulate fixed guidelines for detailed description. These may include the printing of the full colophon, where extant, or at least of all the names of scribe, bishop, etc. They will count quires, note which leaf was replaced or reinked, decipher scribbles, notes of ownership, etc.

The present catalogue has been compiled with greater freedom of description — according to the item described and the interest of this writer. As will be detailed below, the Harvard collection consists of two kinds of manuscripts: a large number of 19th century copies — often specially prepared for the European or American missionary or scholar — and a smaller number of ancient codices. As a rule, the recent copies contain lengthy colophons which are of little interest to anyone but to those who look for a very special type of information.[14] On the other hand, very few of the ancient codices have kept their colophons. To be sure, information from ancient colophons has been treated differently.As a rule, beyond a certain set pattern of minimum information (see below), freedom of description is evident throughout. Much optional information is included and it

---

[13] So far no one has done for Baumstark what Fuat Sezgin did for Brockelmann. This is an appropriate occasion to put forward the suggestion that an International Board of scholars should meet for planning a complete index of all the works known to exist in Syriac MSS. Such tools are available today for Hebrew and Arabic, covering at least a large part of the material. It is time that students of Syriac will have the same kind of tool, the more so since in recent years the treasures remaining in churches and monasteries in Turkey, Iraq, etc. have been largely listed. I hope that some Academy will shoulder the financial burden of such an enterprise.

[14] I did not feel constrained to offer information to students of 19th century scribal workshops. The information "complete" will mean that readers stand a good chance to get some kind of information out of the colophon, if they care to study it.

mirrors, to some extent, personal interests.[15] This is one of the privileges I conferred upon myself — I assume most catalogues prepared by visitors will roughly follow the same trail of freedom.[16]

While it is hazardous to speculate on the future, one characteristic of this catalogue may be pointed out. It is the first catalogue which describes a Syriac collection in America. It is no coincidence that America does not boast Syriac collections of importance, even though the overall number of MSS which found their way to American libraries is impressive.[17] But for some unusual stroke of luck, American libraries never stood a chance of acquiring the kind of collection that could be assembled in European centers before the first despatches of manuscripts from the Urmia mission ever reached American shores. Since present day whereabouts of Syriac MSS in the West are pretty well known, it would seem that this first catalogue of a large American collection of

---

[15] In general, the information deals with the literary units involved, identifying as much as possible. Owners' notes, scribbles, etc. were usually left out, and so were descriptions of illuminations. The latter was possible, because at the time of finalizing this catalogue, Dr. Lawrence Nees is working on a detailed description of some of the more important illuminated or ornamented MSS, i.e., MSS Syr 2 and 4. Students of illuminations will usually find no more than a general remark in my catalogue. As it happens, MSS Syr 2 and 4 contain some unusual features, such as horizontally drawn coloured figures of two Evangelists, or ornamental crosses in beginning and end (with inscriptions possibly having some "guardian" aspect), etc. My attempts to decipher the writing will be included in Dr. Nees' paper.

[16] To be sure, there is a difference if a visitor encounters a large collection or if he runs into a few items. Cf. the recent description by S. Brock, "The Syriac MSS in the National Library of Athens," *Muséon* 79 (1966) 165 f. One MS has been announced for Innsbruck by Grill, *Oriens Christ* 52 (1968) 152 f., etc. Cf. also *List of Old Testament Peshitta Manuscripts* (1961) 56.

[17] If we take Clemons' list as a basis, the number will probably reach the neighborhood of 500. This is still less than the holdings of one major European library, like the Vatican or the British Library.

14

Syriac codices will also be the last.[18] On the other hand, the announcements of Vööbus[19] and Macomber[20] whet our appetite as to what may be yet expected from churches, monasteries, etc. in the Middle East.[21]

Because of the way the Harvard collection was assembled, I decided to publish appendices on two additional American collections. For it was partly the same sources that also fed the library of the Harvard Divinity School and of the Union Theological Seminary in New York. There is definitely a problem regarding descriptions that appeared about a century ago in the learned American journals of the day (mainly by Isaac Hall). We remain in some doubt as to where each item went. Including the holdings of those libraries in this volume should help to clarify things.[22] It should be stressed that

[18] The only sizeable collection in the West still uncatalogued is the one housed in the John Rylands Library in Manchester. According to my notations it consists of about seventy codices, apart from some "rotographs." Cf. my remarks in *Bulletin of the John Rylands Library* 37 (1955) 429 f. Dr. J.H. Charlesworth of Duke University has written to inform me that he intends to publish a catalogue. Syriac holdings of European libraries were indexed a generation ago by Jean Simon, "Repertoire des bibliothéques publiques et privées d'Europe contenant des manuscrits syriaques," Or 9 (1940) 271 f.

[19] For various announcements cf. the notes in his recent introduction to *The Pentateuch in the Version of the Syro-Hexapla, CSCC* 369 (1975). Vööbus has announced his intention to publish an entire series: *Catalogues of Syriac Manuscripts in unknown collections in the Syrian Orient;* Cf. *JAOS* 96 (1976) 577; [*JNES* 37 (1978) 190].

[20] *ZDMG, Suppl* 1 (1969) 473 f.

[21] It stands to reason that some of the codices which came to Harvard may turn out to be stemmatically related to MSS still kept in such church libraries. Of course, those MSS copied a century ago in Urmia from a *Vorlage* in the "College" must now be used instead of the destroyed originals. Note also the paper of Helga Anschütz, *ZDMG* ib, p. 500.

[22] Note the opening paragraphs for each appendix. Given the nature of this catalogue as a whole, I had no intention of getting involved in more and more issues. The appendices are therefore no more than handlists.

whereas these collections were partly fed by the same sources, there was never any direct administrative connection. The two Harvard collections have different histories, and share only a name in common.[23] All in all, this volume deals with about 230 items, one-half of the Syriac holdings of all American libraries taken together.

IV

The origin and fate of each codex in the Harvard collection has been given in detail. Some remarks are in order as to how the collection was built, as a whole.

Over two-thirds of the collection belonged to J. Rendell Harris and came to Harvard in one lot. The student of Syriac who moves from one library to another will realise, how Harris collected and sold or donated and then collected again and sold again.[24] Some of the manuscripts collected by Harris were old codices, though hardly ever in perfect shape and usually lacking the colophon. Many items were recent copies, usually — though not always — especially prepared for him. All

---

[23] Clemons' wording (p. 23) may be misleading when he states: "Most of the MSS now at Harvard are held in the Houghton library, although a few are found in the Andover-Harvard Theological Library." For an item that got into a third Harvard collection cf. Appendix I. In this catalogue the term "Harvard Collection" will only be used as regards manuscripts now kept at Houghton. The Library of the Divinity School will always be referred to as Andover-Harvard (AH).

[24] One can find codices which, belonged to Harris in libraries like John Rylands, Haverford, Pierpont Morgan and Clare College. In *Bulletin John Rylands* 37:430 I have already had some difficulty with the fate of a Harris MS. For a long time a Syriac MS numbered 1 was deemed to be missing from Harvard. The truth is that that MS never came to Harvard in the first place — it was No. 1 in Harris' list, but was not part of the deal with Harvard. Allowing for MSS which never came to Harvard and some erroneous duplicate numbers, I assume that the Harvard-Harris collection contained 125 volumes.

16

Harris codices bear his bookplate with a line from Keats: "Then felt I like some watcher of the skies when a new planet swims into his ken" — the text illustrated with an appropriate drawing. Many codices can be recognized because they were specially bound by Wilson in Cambridge.

There is no reason to assume but that Harris collected for his own personal interest and use. In any event he did not lose by selling. Since European libraries were well supplied around 1900, it was natural that he looked for a buyer in America. Thus the Semitic Museum at Harvard, then recently established, became the owner of a collection which was respectable by European standards, although definitely second class.[25]

The majority of the Harris codices come from the same source as other Harvard Syriac MSS, i.e., the mission in Urmia (Oroomiah). It almost seems as if part of the economic basis of the mission station consisted in running some kind of copying service for scholars.[26] The same kind of copy finally

[25] Quite some time after the deal with the Semitic Museum was closed, other Harris manuscripts appeared on the market. Those, however,seem to have been offered through trade channels and were not picked up by Harvard. In any event, when I checked the holdings of the Pierpont Morgan library in New York, back in 1960, I noticed that their MSS M 783 and M 784 came from Harris. Cf. the report *The Pierpont Morgan Library — Review of the Activities and Acquisitions of the Library for 1930 through 1935* (1935) 15. See also Casey, *JTS* 2 (1951) 65. (Those MSS were also bound by Wilson.) My notes indicate that I tracked those volumes down to an offer in Catalogue 50 (1934) of Wm. H. Robinson of London. The price mentioned was £2500, whereas the entire collection sold to Harvard thirty years earlier fetched £1350 (see note 29, below). Perhaps this is some kind of consolation to a generation suffering from chronic inflation.

As for the two other MSS of the Syriac New Testament at Pierpont Morgan, cf. below No. 45. We can thus account for the provenance of all Syriac MSS in an additional American collection (apart from the one leaf M 774).

[26] Shedd had access to good MSS in the library of the "College." The catalogue prepared by Shedd (together with Oshana Saru) almost shared the fate of the Urmi collection itself. It is extremely

17

reached Harvard via the American Board of Commissioners for Foreign Missions, via direct contacts between Shedd and the Semitic Museum[27] via Harris and via Hall. There are enough letters in various volumes to show that Harris was in close contact with W.A. Shedd and that Shedd arranged for most of the copying.[28]

The Harris collection got to the Semitic Museum by purchase, as indicated in the accession notice of November 3, 1905.[29] It was purely a sale transaction, although Harris toyed with the idea of going with his collection to America. Harris kept a few MSS with him in Selly Oak, because he happened to be working on them. Hence his MSS Nos. 41, 83, 130 were sent to Harvard only during World War I (March 1915). Once the collection was sold, there was little further contact, but Harris decided later on to offer one set of notes as a donation.[30] Together with the collection came a handlist of a few pages which has served, in a way, all later users.[31]

difficult to discover a copy and to get an idea of the MSS kept in that library. Cf. *Catalogue of Syriac MSS in the Library of the Museum Association of Oroomiah College* (1898).

[27]   Cf. note on MS Syr 156.

[28]   Cf. note on MS Syr 92. From a letter written by Shedd to Harris (April 1899) it is clear that their correspondence touched on various subjects of common scholarly interest — among them the famous concordance to the Peshitta (which was also ultimately destroyed).

[29]   While the inventory lists were available, the archive material of the Semitic Museum was only recently arranged so as to be used. In 1977, I could finally study the correspondence between Harris and Moore which had led to the purchase. On August 24, 1905 Harris accepted the Harvard offer and the collection was sold for £1350 — which equalled $6750. The sum of $1500 was contributed by Schiff. Originally Harris demanded £1700, as a price for his Syriac as well as his Armenian manuscripts.

[30]   This is now MS Syr 179. This was offered by Harris in a letter dated February 7, 1916. Also later on (January, 1925), when Titterton was puzzled by a volume, he would write to Harris for an explanation; cf. note on MS Syr 92.

[31]   It seems that the original list was the basis for Clemons' descriptions.

18

If we look at the list of accessions of the Semitic Museum it is obvious that the Harris collection was by far the most important acquisition since its beginning.[32] It was therefore somewhat amazing that in the official description of the activities of the Museum, the matter is not even mentioned.[33] As remarked above, the Harris collection was the major component of the acquisitions by the Semitic Museum, but not the only one. Some MSS came from sources connected with the Urmia mission; some were bought from estates of scholars (especially Hall and Moore); some were chance gifts.[34]

In greater detail: The very first items noted in the list of accessions (under March 17, 1890) were Syriac manuscripts.[35] First among those was what is now MS Syr 141.[36] Soon after came MS 142[37] and then MSS 137–138.[38] The next major acquisition came from the estate of Isaac Hall, entered in 1900 as SM access 2175 ff.[39] Five years later the Harris

---

[32] Harvard almost missed the opportunity. Harris had set a "refusal deadline" which Harvard had not kept. Thereupon he offered the collection to Yale. But at the time Professor Bacon was away and no one at Yale could act on the offer. Meanwhile Harvard agreed — and the deal was carried out.

[33] Professor D.G. Lyon, who was himself active with regard to acquisition, wrote the chapter concerning the Semitic Museum, which appeared in S.E. Morison, *The Development of Harvard University 1869–1929* (1930) 231 f.

[34] Cf. notes on MS Syr 136, 156, 176. When Titterton listed the holdings half a century ago, he counted 136 items.

[35] Items 2–8. Item 1 was an "architectonic model."

[36] Actually MS SM access 841 "a gift of Thomas Laurie" was given to Harvard before the rest of the MSS (December 19, 1889), but it got to SM only in the spring of 1890.

[37] Cf. a letter by Emily Burleigh, dated March 28, 1890.

[38] A first short description was given by Lyon in *JAOS* 15 (1893) ci; cf. note on MS Syr 142.

[39] As noted above (end of III) MSS that belonged to Hall can be found in different American collections. Hall was the most competent student of Syriac literature in America in the late 19th century, and he was quite a collector. But his collection could not rival the Harris collection; Cf. No. 51.

collection was purchased. The last Syriac items to come to SM were access 8375–77, now MS Syr 171–173.[40]

The entire collection of Syriac MSS was moved from the Semitic Museum in various lots to the Houghton library. This began fairly soon after Houghton was opened. Houghton was intended as a place to care for rare books and MSS, and the SM was not geared to render library services.

Also the American Board of Commissioners for Foreign Missions[41] had decided — back in 1942 — to deposit its holdings in Houghton. These are the MSS now numbered MS Syr 2–13.[42]

From the point of view of Houghton: The A B C F M manuscripts came in 1942. In 1944 the first lot was transferred from SM, but no accessions numbers were given before 1955.[43] These are now MS Syr 14–22. The bulk of the SM collection was transferred in 1959, but none of those MSS received an additional Houghton accessions number.

By the time I came to Harvard in 1960 all manuscripts had just been assembled in Houghton, and — quite unknown to me — it was the right time to try and get some order into the collection. Some "forgotten" MSS were transferred from SM in 1970, when I was working on the pre-final draft. For the strange fate of MS Syr 176, cf. *ad loc.* The collection as it

---

[40] The accession notes for those fragments (July 19, 1922) show that at that time Titterton was already writing on Syriac MSS.
[41] These will be referred to as A B C F M items.
[42] As far as I can make out, these were deposited, not donated. This means that none of the MSS kept at Houghton as the Harvard Syriac collection actually "belongs" to the library. The exceptions are MS Syr 1, 136, for these are original Harvard College Library items. In fact, MS Syr 1 is the first Syriac MS that came to Harvard (1863).
[43] According to the Houghton lists, labelling took place in 1957 only. The reason may be that only then it seemed certain that the depositing was a permanent arrangement. The labels then attached read: Harvard College Library.

stands now was renumbered by the Houghton curator in 1970, and these numbers should be used in the future.[44]

<h1 style="text-align:center">V</h1>

The Harvard Syriac collection consists at present of 179 items. Exactly half of these are MSS copied in the late 18th or 19th century, right up to the time when Harris sold his collection. About 25 items are comparatively old, i.e., mainly 12–13th century or slightly older. There is not even one codex which may be said to belong to the early period, i.e., 6th–8th century, and practically all old codices are incomplete. About 18 items are comparatively old fragments, one leaf or more. Again, almost all belong to the 12th–13th centuries, but a few may go back to the 7th. About a quarter of the MSS are from the period between the 14th and 18th centuries.

Most of the older codices are either manuscripts of the Bible or of the prayerbook. Only one item (MS Syr 176) is of unique interest in the field of Syriac manuscripts, as a whole. Our study shows that the first half of Harris' collection contained an appreciably higher percentage of older MSS than the second half.

If we try to evaluate collections, *grosso modo,* the Harvard collection comes way behind the great collections of European centers like Rome, Paris, London. This comparison would be unfair. Nor does it compare with Berlin, Cambridge or Selly Oak, although it is not dissimilar typologically. On the other hand, once we get beyond the big first ten, it compares well

---

[44] Cf. n. 9. Orders should quote the exact shelfmark, as given in Mr. Dennis' appended list. For instance, item 12 of this catalogue should be ordered as: fMS Syriac 12; item 110 as pfMS Syriac 110, etc. To prevent unnecessary queries: as stated above, Clemons did not study the MSS, but used the old Harris list. Items 159 and 161 as listed by Clemons (SM access 4058, 4060) were already missing in 1960 — Clemons simply was not aware of the fact. I do not know when these MSS disappeared — it is some consolation that they are modern copies.

with second class European collections and outranks many of them.

It would be difficult to put a price tag on such a collection. In the late 19th century a MS of about 100 leaves could be produced for five dollars, as we see in a note in MS Syr 178. On the other hand, two old codices (MS Syr 137, 138) were acquired for $100.– perhaps because these were defective or because of Moore's position Harvard got those MSS from the estate at a low price. Compared with these figures, the price of $6750 for the entire Harris collection in 1905 seems low — even if we reckon today's values about 1:100.[45] All in all, if such a collection were for sale today, the price would easily top one million dollars and might run as high as two million.

VI

The procedure adopted in this catalogue is flexible and eclectic and, as set out above, does not note every detail consistently. Texts have been identified, to the best of my ability, or else *incipits* were given so that others might do better. It goes without saying that I used whatever previous information was available.[46] Scholars who happen to have in their possession a copy of any previous description will find a considerable number of differences. Except for misprints and mishaps, discrepancies between this catalogue and previous

---

[45] Among my notes I find a reference to the fact that when around that time Torrey tried to persuade the Yale Library to buy a MS of the Syriac N.T., he suggested that the copy might be purchased for $300 — instead of the $500 asked for. See the letter attached to what is now Yale Syriac 6. That is, of course, an older and complete N.T. Torrey mentioned on that occasion that two other MSS from that source had been purchased by Pierpont Morgan. On the other hand, we have mentioned already the price of $2,500 paid for two MSS of the N.T. in 1934 (Cf. n. 25).

[46] A few details are offered in Titterton's (=Ti) name; these were not checked. Titterton in his dissertation drafts followed the Wright method and, for instance, copied out the arrangement of weekly lessons from a lectionary. Such details are not given in this catalogue, and Titterton's draft remains useful.

notations are intentional. However, only in rare circumstances has such a discrepancy been commented upon.[47]

As a rule, I have included references only to what is not obvious or not easily available and I have refrained from copying out what is entered *s.v.* in sources like Baumstark and Moss.[48] Relevant journals were checked for material not yet included in *SPB*, roughly from the end-fifties on.[49] While I tried to refer to publications which have a direct bearing on the text included in the MSS described, exhaustiveness in references is not the aim of this volume.[50] Previous mention of

---

[47] This excludes specifically the issue of foliation. Many MSS were foliated by Harris or others, in part incorrectly. As a rule, I neither rewrote numbers of leaves nor did I enter new numbers into the MSS. I am neither the owner of the collection nor its keeper. It stands to reason that with all the recounting there will be mistakes and I am far from satisfied with the absolute exactness of my count.

[48] A. Baumstark, *Geschichte der Syrischen Literatur* (1922) = *GSL*; C. Moss, *Catalogue of Syriac Printed Books and related Literature in the British Museum* (1962) = *SPB*. Recent "Histories of Syriac Literature", published in Cairo and Bagdad, possess little independent value. Items from the British Museum (= BM) are sometimes referred to by the new name of that institution, i.e., British Library. A fairly comprehensive list of bibliographical aids and listings is given by J.T. Clemons, *An Index of Syriac MSS containing the epistles and the apocalypse, Studies and Documents* (ed. J. Geerlings) 38 (1968).

[49] I am aware of omissions in *SPB*, as pointed out at the time in reviews. The publications checked for possibly relevant materials are: *Muséon, Oriens Christianus, Orientalia Christiana (Analecta et Periodica), L'Orient Syrien*. As for the series, *CSCO*, (*Corpus Scriptorum Christianorum Orientalium — Scriptores Syri*) is of prime importance. Some references come from *Patrologia Orientalis*. In recent years, publications have come from the *Göttinger Arbeitskreis für Syrische Kirchengeschichte*. Note also the relevant sections in *ZDMG, Suppl* 1 (1969). The proceedings of the Rome meeting have been collected in *OCA* 1974, but they are of little interest for this volume.

[50] As in most fields, some publications of interest appear in non-specialized places. Thus, only by chance I saw G. Wiessner, "Untersuchungen zur Syrischen Literaturgeschichte 1," *Abhlg. Akad. Wiss. Göttingen, Phil-Hist. KL 111, 67* (1967) and his "Zur Hand-

MSS from the Harvard collection has been noted, wherever possible. There will be found some differences between the attention given at the time to the early acquisitions[51] and to those which were studied by Harris and later scholars.[52]

Some remarks on dating and terminology are in order. The connoisseurs of Syriac in past generations possessed a sound knowledge of writers and writings as well as of manuscripts. I am not saying that we know nothing about the nature of Syriac MSS, but such knowledge is hardly the result of scientific study. It was acquired as a matter of intuition and impression. This is no reflection on paleography and related

---

schriftenüberlieferung der syrischen Fassung des Corpus Dyonysiacum," *ib* 1972. Note also the publication by some scholars who have recently begun to revive the British tradition of Syriac learning, such as S. Brock, R.Y. Ebied, L.R. Wickham. To be sure, some of that work is connected to the MSS of the Mingana collection; cf. recently R. Degen, *JSS* 1972: 213.

[51] Some items were described between 1875 and 1890 in the *Proceedings of the American Oriental Society* and (what was to become) the *Journal of Biblical Literature*. Those descriptions were mostly by Isaac H. Hall (cf. above, n. 39 and MS Syr 3). Note also *Hebraica* 8:132; *Presbyterian Review* 7:537. Hall's papers are the mainstay of Clemons' "Supplement Americain au Syriac Catalogue de Cyril Moss," *L'Orient Syrien* 8 (1963) 469 f. Early references to MSS of the N.T. in C.R. Gregory, *Textkritik des N.T.* (1902) go back to Hall's notices. For a description of a certain part of the early Harvard collection cf. note on MS Syr 156. Perkins described his encounter with Syriac MSS in early volumes of the *American Biblical Repository* (1837, 1841, etc.). As far as I can see, these have no bearing on Harvard MSS. On the history of how the MSS became available for the missionaries in Urmi — ultimately serving as *Vorlage* for a good many MSS in our collection — cf. J. Perkins *Residence of Eight Years in Persia* (1843).

[52] Harris discussed some MSS before the collection was sold. Cf. notes on MSS Syr 54, 70, 75, 81, 95, 137. Leading students of Syriac half a century ago dealt with certain items (cf. MSS Syr 64, 119, 125) and recent listings of MSS for certain subjects — like those of Vööbus and Macomber and Brock — contain references. Cf. now *OCP* 36 (1970) 120 f.; *JSS* 14 (1969) 207; 211.

fields in general; it is a statement on the state of the art with regard to Syriac MSS.

The author of a catalogue of Syriac MSS can either be prudent or informative. If he is prudent he keeps silent — apart from those few cases where he has a colophon in front of him. If he wants to be informative, he will attempt dating — possibly doing little more than giving proof of his ignorance.[53]

My only consolation is that I am not alone in my ignorance. There are very few people alive today who have enough experience to date the holdings of a Syriac collection, and I do not think that anyone has developed objective criteria.[54] Once the study of Syriac MSS is put on a sounder basis,[55] datings may have to be revised. In any event, I have looked at

---

[53] We shall have occasion to deal with the problem of MS Syr 176, alleged to be the oldest codex written in Serto. I should add that if I were to date the oldest dated codex written in Estrangelo (BM Add 12150), I would never dare to suggest ca 400 C.E. Thus, e.g., if the analysis of possible allographic distribution of connected and disconnected letters *r* and *d* in Syriac leads in any direction, I would opt for later rather than earlier dating. By the same token, BM Add 14425 which is half a century later than Add 12150, turns out earlier upon paleographic analysis. Which shows how little ductus dating can be relied upon. Incidentally, I have some difficulty with hand and wording of the decisive information fol 115*b*; but I am reluctant to cast doubts on colophons without decisive proof.

[54] One has to be both inexperienced and unjustifiably optimistic in order to assume that problems can be solved with the aid of W.H.P. Hatch, *An Album of Dated Syriac Manuscripts* (Boston, 1946).

[55] I assume that a proper typology will finally be based on codicology rather than on the study of *ductus*. To my knowledge, nobody has ever seriously tried to typologize Syriac codices. Originally I had intended to render an exact account of quires, layers, etc. as a contribution to future study. The state of most of the older MSS in the collection, however, is such that a proper description would have meant such an investment of time that this catalogue would have never been published. In consequence, I have decided to drop all such references. Generally speaking, Syriac MSS are arranged in *quiniones;* it is the *quaterniones* that have to be watched.

so many thousands of Syriac MSS in my lifetime that I thought I might give my very subjective suggestions of dating for what they are worth.

Whereas the problem of dating is to be expected, one would have imagined that over the past hundred years clear criteria have been established as to the typology of MSS. I have used a purely formal type of labelling, i.e., I do not label the MS as a whole but the script. *Serto*[56] refers always to Western cursive, unless qualified in a very special case, as commented upon *ad loc*. Hence, a MS written in *Serto* may be presumed to be "Western" (see note 58). *Estrangelo* refers always to the fully non-cursive form, and secondary indication (liturgy, author, vocalization, etc.) will be decisive as regards possible Western or Eastern character). Many MSS, especially of a liturgical character, written around 1200, which are often termed *Estrangelo* but actually show cursive ("Sertoid") forms of the letters *d, r, h,* have been classified as *Cursive Estrangelo*.[57] Since this script leans towards Serto forms, I had in some cases to label *Nestorian Cursive Estrangelo*. Apart from a few items characterized as *Melkite* (see *ad loc*), all remaining MSS are classified as *Nestorian*.[58]

---

[56] I have not "Easternized" these terms. It is mainly Serto MSS that I have characterized with some reluctance as "inelegant," "semi-professional," etc.

[57] As the years went by, I have tried different terms: Cursive, Jacobite, Liturgical Estrangelo. Looking back at *Bulletin John Rylands* 37:435, I realize that I must have encountered that same problem a quarter of a century ago.

[58] I have avoided *Jacobite,* but not *Nestorian,* although authorities of both sides have strenuously objected to the terms. I could not get used to writing "Eastern" instead of "Nestorian," although for the sake of consistency I should have. If a Nestorian MS is vocalized, it is by definition Nestorian vocalization, and need not be stated. As a matter of fact, almost all recent Nestorian MSS are at least partly vocalized. If a Serto MS is vocalized, it is stated what vocalization is used — the same goes for some vocalized Estrangelo MSS. The "Greek" vocalization is termed *Western,* so that the term "Jacobite" is not used at all.

This last section of the Introduction will deal with the layout of the descriptions and with some of the remaining technical problems of the catalogue.

Each manuscript has been identified by its present number, which is the only one relevant for ordering and quoting. In brackets, I have added earlier references. Those may relate to the accession number of the Semitic Museum or Houghton, to the numbering of Harris and Clemons, to the page in Titterton's dissertation, or some partial listing. Most codices have a SMH number which means: a Semitic Museum manuscript numbered according to the Harris collection.[59] Accession numbers following SMH refer to the Semitic Museum listing, unless otherwise specified.

Identification is followed by a summarizing description of the contents of each codex, printed in capitals. This summary may refer to author and book, to Bible or Prayer Book, to a "collection" type, etc. As far as possible, stereotypes have been employed, but slight differences of formulation do not indicate difference of substance.[60] All matters of detail are left for the second section of the description, headed *Details.*

After the summarizing description, the date is given. It goes without saying that *ductus*-dating is only resorted to if no colophon date survives. Dates are given in the original notation of the Greek calendar (indicated: Sel), unless the MS gives only C.E. dates. I have added the month, where indicated, in order to oblige those who wish to subtract

---

[59] Ti = Titterton; Cl = Clemons; Go = Goshen-Gottstein, *Textus* 2:52; PM = *List of Old Testament Peshitta Manuscripts* (1961). For a major part of the catalogue SMH numbers are described in sequence by Titterton, and no Ti reference has to be given.

[60] I may have "over-stereotyped" by using "Book of Prayer and Services," partly in order not to get involved in problems of liturgical differentiation for which I am absolutely unqualified. Note the terms in the introduction to Wright's BM catalogue, p. XVIII.

correctly 311 or 312, as the case may be.[61] Dating by ductus is indicated, e.g., "ca 15 cent" or "15–16 cent."

As noted above, information on places, monasteries, bishops, etc. is added from ancient colophons only. Only in a few cases have I remarked on information contained in 19 cent colophons. As a rule, these will have to wait for someone interested in digesting that kind of material.

The next item in the description concerns script and vocalization. As the case may be, terms like "partly," "mixed vocal," etc. need no explanation.[62] Because of the special interest, the relatively few MSS which indicate *kušāyā* and *rukākhā* have been remarked upon by the term "spirant."

If the MS is written in two columns it has been noted; writing in three columns is practically nonexistent. Lines have not been counted. All counting is done by *leaves,* and in accordance with widespread usage indications are, e.g., *5a* — not *5r.* If European, Arabic or Syriac pagination exists in the codex, it has been noted.[63]

---

[61] I am aware of the remarks of F. Ludger Bernhard, *Die Chronologie der Syrischen Handschriften* (1971), but I admit that I find his elaboration on the subject a bit tiring. The reckoning of the Greek era starts 1 October 312 B.C.E., and if someone wishes to avoid the mistakes enumerated by Bernhard my notation should help him.

[62] A relatively large number of 19th century MSS in the collection are written in Serto with "mixed vocalization." I do not know of any attempt to gain systematic knowledge.

[63] Because of the many unnumbered leaves there will be mistakes, and I am afraid that at some later date the manuscripts will be foliated, not in accordance with the description. As a rule, empty leaves have been counted only if there were more than two. Such empty leaves are numbered in brackets e.g. 57 (+5) fol. Numbers in brackets refer almost always to leaves in the end of the MS, but some MSS have a number of leaves in the beginning, and those were counted as well (not separately). Hence the numbering in a MS like MS Syr 115 will appear odd. In any event, scholars who order microfilms are well advised to order always a few additional pages, just in case.

In 1977, all measurements were rewritten in cm (but not in mm). All measurements refer to the leaf as a whole, not to the written part.

After the measurements the description indicates the material, paper or vellum. These may be qualified, such as: European paper, wavy vellum. The notation "complete" indicates that the MS has been preserved without loss of its final leaves; this means usually that a colophon exists. "Complete" does not indicate the amount of possible damage to the MS, missing leaves, etc. Such damage is referred to separately, in a general way.

Where applicable, details on illumination and binding are given.[64] Finally, items may be added to the description to indicate, e.g., the source of a Houghton codex — such as A B C F M (cf. note 41). Comparison to other MSS in the collection can also come at this point — or else in a note. As a rule, the index should be checked for such matters.

The units enumerated so far belong to the "basic" description of each Harvard manuscript.[65] All other facts have been enumerated as *Details* or are remarked upon in the *Notes,* as the case may be. Details of units in a volume are given according to a certain stereotype. Thus, e.g., beginning leaves of books of the Old Testament are indicated — because there are only MSS of parts of the O.T. in the collection. On the other hand, volumes of the New Testament detail the *incipits* of the Gospels, Acts, James and Hebrews only.

For typographical reasons, Syriac has been used in the *Notes* only. As much as feasible I have transliterated. The transliteration is very broadly phonetic, but I have not corrected all inconsistencies, and I do not think that "problems" such as

---

[64] Cf. n. 15. I am not qualified to evaluate the information included in J. Leroy, *Les Manuscrits Syriaques a peintures conservés dans les bibliothéques d'Europe et d'Orient* (1964). The only binding of interest is that of MS Syr 176.

[65] AH and UTS manuscripts follow the guidelines, but according to the character of those lists, the flexibility is greater.

š/sh are of vital importance as regards this catalogue. Hence, by the time this is printed the same author may appear as 'Abd-Īšō'/Isho', etc., but I did not follow a spelling such as Moss': 'Abhd. Again, although some traditionally standardized names remain, Ebedjesus is gone. I am used to Aphrem — not Ephraim, Efrem, Ephrem, etc.

All identifications are *prima facie*. Only when a certain work is more or less generally acknowledged to be wrongly ascribed, the description will refer to that fact. Terms like discourses, epistles, hymns, tracts, etc. are used as stereotypes, not as fixed equivalents for Syriac terms.[66]

All texts are presumed to be written in Syriac, unless otherwise specified. The collection contains a high proportion of writings in Modern Syriac, most of those in "standardized Urmi" or in the language of surrounding villages.[67] Manuscripts written partly or entirely in Garshuni[68] have been described as such. There exists no accepted term for texts in Turkish, Persian, etc., written in Syriac letters. In light of Malabar *Gerisoni* I hope a term like "Turkish Garshuni" will at least be understood.[69]

In light of what has been said about the nature of this

---

[66] I realized too late that I should have stuck to Syriac terms and written *mēmrā* , etc. As is happens, *mēmrā* is rendered "discourse," but "discourse" is not solely the equivalent of *mēmrā*.

[67] Concerning the terminology, cf. the recent summary by I. Avinery, *Afroasiatic Linguistics* 2 (1976) 201. We may have, indeed, one example of a text in the Zakho Jewish dialect, as dictated to a Christian. This needs further dialectological investigation (cf. MS Syr 7). Of linguistic interest is also an exercise of translation from "standardized Urmi" to classical Syriac (MS Syr 9).

[68] I have got used to the form *Garshuni*. Reasons have been reviewed in Hatch's *Album* p. 42. The explanation remains doubtful, but the pronunciation seems accepted.

[69] I am aware of one case of an explicit paraphrase. That is the manuscript written by Moses Mardenus in Latin, using Syriac letters, described (in Garshuni) as: *walḥarf huwa suryānī wal-lafẓ frangī* (Wright, Cat. BM, p. 214).

catalogue there is no point in adding many plates, even if the cost were not prohibitive. The photographs will illustrate some of the problems encountered and some points of special interest. These may be issues of illumination (MSS Syr 2, 20) or text (MS Syr 28) or script (MSS Syr 63, 173) or date (MS Syr 176). All plates should be viewed in conjunction with the description offered.

*   *

*

I started this introduction by remarking on the fact that of all the projects I am engaged in this one was the least likely to be finished. One of the reasons for my doubts was that I am not accustomed any more to working completely on my own, without the benefit of co-workers who can save me from all manner of mishaps, misspellings, misnumberings[70] — and, most important, who can prepare an index. It was a salutary exercise to prepare a volume for which I have to accept the total blame.

My thanks to those who helped with the technical preparation. The manuscript for the printers was typed by Ms. Judith Singer of the Semitic Museum office. Scholars Press agreed to have the type set by my Jerusalem printer, Academic Press. Mr. Shimon Vaknin did a superb job with the new Syriac grid and Mr. Abraham Gino arranged the pages with his usual skill.

Harvard
June 1977   M.H.G.

---

[70] I have noted with distress that I am liable to write 555 when I want to write 444, that I jotted down in my notes Wright, Cambridge — when I meant London, that I wrote 1908 for 1898, Syriaque for Syriac, etc. I can only hope that I tracked down most of these mishaps, which are as irritating to the user as they are embarrassing to the author.

CONCORDANCE OF PRESENT SHELFMARKS
AND PREVIOUS LISTINGS
(cf. Introduction, note 44)

Houghton Library Call Number			Houghton Library Accessions Number	Semitic Museum Harris Number	Semitic Museum Accessions Number	Clemons Number
fMS	Syriac	1				
MS	"	2	*42M-749			8
fMS	"	3	*42M-754			9
MS	"	4	*42M-753			10
MS	"	5	*42M-1690			11
MS	"	6	*42M-1772			12
MS	"	7	*42M-1861			
MS	"	8	*42M-1862			
MS	"	9	*42M-1866			
MS	"	10	*42M-1884			13
MS	"	11	*42M-1883			14
fMS	"	12	*42M-1699			15
MS	"	13	*42M-1865			
MS	"	14	*55M-278	2	3945	52
MS	"	15	*55M-279	94	4029	132
MS	"	16	*55M-280	13	3951	58
MS	"	17	*55M-281	117	4052	153
fMS	"	18	*55M-282	53	3991	98
fMS	"	19	*55M-283	17	3955	62
fMS	"	20	*55M-284	16	3954	61
MS	"	21	*55M-287	114	4049	151
MS	"	22	*55M-288	50	3988	95
MS	"	23		3	3946	53
MS	"	24		4	3947	54
MS	"	25		5	3948	55
MS	"	26		6	3949	56
MS	"	27		7	3950	57
MS	"	28		14	3952	59
fMS	"	29		15	3953	60
fMS	"	30		18	3956	63
fMS	"	31		19	3957	64
fMS	"	32		20	3958	65
fMS	"	33		21	3959	66
MS	"	34		22	3960	67
MS	"	35		23	3961	68
MS	"	36		24	3962	69
MS	"	37		25	3963	70

Houghton Library Call Number			Semitic Museum Harris Number	Semitic Museum Accessions Number	Clemons Number
MS	Syriac	38	26	3964	71
MS	"	39	27	3965	72
MS	"	40	28	3966	73
MS	"	41	29	3967	74
MS	"	42	30	3968	75
MS	"	43	31	3969	76
MS	"	44	32	3970	77
MS	"	45	33	3971	78
MS	"	46	34	3972	79
MS	"	47	35	3973	80
MS	"	48	36	3974	81
MS	"	49	37	3975	82
MS	"	50	38	3976	83
MS	"	51	39	3977	84
MS	"	52	40	3978	85
MS	"	53	41	3979	86
fMS	"	54	42	3980	87
fMS	"	55	43	3981	88
fMS	"	56	44	3982	89
MS	"	57	45	3983	90
MS	"	58	46	3984	91
MS	"	59	47	3985	92
MS	"	60	48	3986	93
fMS	"	61	49	3987	94
MS	"	62	51	3989	96
MS	"	63	52	3990	97
fMS	"	64	54	3992	99
fMS	"	65	55	3993	100
fMS	"	66	56	3994	101
fMS	"	67	57	3995	102
fMS	"	68	58	3996	103
fMS	"	69	59	3997	104
MS	"	70	60	3998	105
MS	"	71	61	3999	106
MS	"	72	62	4000	107
MS	"	73	63	4001	108
MS	"	74	64	4002	109
MS	"	75	65	4003	110
MS	"	76	66	4004	111
MS	"	77	67	4005	112

Houghton Library Call Number			Semitic Museum Harris Number	Semitic Museum Accessions Number	Clemons Number
MS	Syriac	78	68	4006	113
MS	"	79	69	4007	114
MS	"	80	70	4008	115
MS	"	81	71	4009	116
MS	"	82	73	4010	117
MS	"	83	74	4011	118
fMS	"	84	75	4012	119
fMS	"	85	76	4013	120
MS	"	86	77	4014	
MS	"	87	79	4015	121
MS	"	88	80	4016	122
MS	"	89	81	4017	
MS	"	90	82	4018	
fMS	"	91	83	4019	123
MS	"	92	84	4020	124
MS	"	93	85	4021	125
MS	"	94	86	4022	
fMS	"	95	87	4023	126
MS	"	96	88	4024	127
MS	"	97	89	4025	128
MS	"	98	90	4026	129
MS	"	99	91	4027	130
fMS	"	100	92	4028	131
MS	"	101	95	4030	133
fMS	"	102	96	4031	134
fMS	"	103	97	4032	135
MS	"	104	98	4033	
MS	"	105	99	4034	136
MS	"	106	100	4035	137
MS	"	107	101	4036	138
bMS	"	108	102	4037	139
MS	"	109	103	4038	140
pfMS	"	110	104	4039	141
MS	"	111	105	4040	142
fMS	"	112	106	4041	143
fMS	"	113	107	4042	144
MS	"	114	108	4043	145
MS	"	115	109	4044	146
fMS	"	116	110	4045	147
MS	"	117	111	4046	148

34

Houghton Library Call Number			M.G. Number	Semitic Museum Harris Number	Semitic Museum Accessions Number	Clemons Number
fMS	Syriac	118		112	4047	149
MS	"	119		113	4048	150
fMS	"	120		116	4051	
MS	"	121		118	4053	154
fMS	"	122		119	4054	155
MS	"	123		120	4055	156
MS	"	124		121	4056	157
MS	"	125		122	4057	158
MS	"	126		124	4059	160
MS	"	127		126	4061	162
MS	"	128		127	4062	163
MS	"	129		128	4063	164
fMS	"	130		129	4064	165
fMS	"	131		130	4065	166
MS	"	132		131	4066	167
fMS	"	133		132	4067	168
fMS	"	134		133	4068	169
MS	"	135		134	4069	170
MS	"	136	501			174
bMS	"	137	502		1076	18
bMS	"	138	503		1077	19
pfMS	"	139	504		2198	20
pfMS	"	140	505		2199	21
fMS	"	141	506		2	22
fMS	"	142	507		43	17
bMS	"	143	508		2190	47
bMS	"	144	509		2188	45
bMS	"	145	510		2189	46
bMS	"	146	512		2191	48
bMS	"	147	514		2193	49
bMS	"	148	515		2194	50
bMS	"	149	516		2195	51
MS	"	150	517		1186	28
bMS	"	151	518		2184	41
bMS	"	152	519		2183	40
bMS	"	153	520		2175	32
bMS	"	154	521		2176	33
bMS	"	155	522		1187	29
bMS	"	156	523		3	23
bMS	"	157	524		1189	31
bMS	"	158	525		6	26

Houghton Library Call Number	Houghton Library Accessions Number	M.G. Number	Semitic Museum Accessions Number	Clemons Number
bMS Syriac 159		526	5	25
bMS " 160		527	2181	38
bMS " 161		528	2180	37
bMS " 162		529	4	24
bMS " 163		530	2182	39
bMS " 164		531	2185	42
bMS " 165		532	7	27
bMS " 166		533	2186	43
bMS " 167		534	2187	44
bMS " 168		535	2177	34
bMS " 169		536	2179	36
bMS " 170		537	2178	35
bMS " 171		550	8375	171
bMS " 172		551	8376	172
bMS " 173		552	8777	173
bMS " 174			1188	30
fMS " 175	*42M-1867F			16
bMS " 176		115 (Harris no.)	4050	152
bMS " 177			841	
bMS " 178			2192	
bMS " 179			8255–8278	

Syr 1   [formerly: Syr 1 F* of Harvard College Library]

MEDICAL PRESCRIPTIONS AND TREATMENTS ("FOLK-MEDICINE"),
WRITTEN IN GARSHUNI; 18–19 century; inelegant Serto; 240
fol; 31 × 21 cm; paper; incomplete; gift of Dr. Isaac
Brinkerkoff of Cambridge, July 10, 1863 — hence the earliest
Syriac manuscript to get into a Harvard collection.

Details: Two hands; fol 1–10 contain treatise (partly illegible),
apparently entitled *wasiyyat salmān alḥakīm wagairih min
alḥukamā alḥādiqīn;*[1] main treatise starts fol 21*b* = 11*b*, based
i.a. on alleged excerpts from writings attributed to Solomon,
Luqman, Galen, Hippocrates, etc., entitled *kunnāš fī aṭṭib;*[2]
special mention made in the introduction of treatment of
women's sterility (*muʿālaǧat anniswān alʿawāqir*); previously
mistakenly identified as 'Treatise on the Syriac Language'
(thus label on binding and Macomber).[3]

[1]   ܩܕܝܫܐ ܐܠܗܝܐ ܡ̈ܢ ܐܚܪ̈ܢܐ ܘܡ̈ܝܩܪܐ ܐܠܗܝܐ ܐܠܡܐ ܩܕܝܫܐ

[2]   ܟܬܒܐ ܦܝ ܐܠܛܒ

[3]   Since this was the first manuscript to come to a Harvard library
one may venture the guess that the label did not refer to more than
'A Treatise in the Syriac Language'. Library card entries of this type
in the Andover-Harvard library favor such an assumption.

Syr 2   [formerly: Houghton Syr 2, access *42M-749; Cl 8]

THE GOSPELS IN THE PESHITTA RECENSION; ca 12 cent; cursive
Estrangelo; 2 col; 135 fol; 15 × 10 cm; vellum; complete; old
Oriental wood and leather binding; some crude illustrations of
Evangelists;[1] A B C F M; according to note on last fol by Dr.
A. Grant the volume was acquired in Mosul.

Details: Mark 40*b;* Luke 64*a;* John 103*a;* Eusebian canons and
some lectionary divisions noted; vellum in wavy condition; last
5 fol added paper, Serto, Adar 1986 Sel.

[1]   Cf. Introduction, n. 15.

Syr 3 [formerly: Houghton Syr 3, access *42M–754F; Cl 9]

NESTORIAN LECTIONARY FROM THE PAULINE EPISTLES ('APOS-TOLOS') IN THE PESHITTA RECENSION ARRANGED FOR SUNDAYS, FESTIVAL DAYS, ETC;[1] Ab 1527 Sel at the monastery of Mar Michael; Estrangelo; partly Nestorian vocal; 2 col; 111 fol; 34 × 24 cm; paper; complete; Arabic and Syriac fragments in cardboard binding; A B C F M; according to note on fly-leaf "obtained by Messrs. Smith and Dwight, American missionaries, from a Nestorian Cathedral Church at Janalava in the province of Oormia, in Persia, A.D. 1831."

Details: Described by Isaac H. Hall, *JBL* 8 (1888) 1 f; hence the statement in C.R. Gregory, *Textkritik des neuen Testamentes II* (1902) 522;[2] colophon slightly damaged; cf. W. Bauer, *Der Apostolos der Syrer* (1903); Macomber has noted that the pericopes in this manuscript do not follow the usual Nestorian tradition, but are similar to the division in the Leningrad MS described *RB* 47 (1938) no 21; details need rechecking.

[1] ܪܒܐ ܗܕܐ ܕܝܠܗ ܗܠܝܢ ܐܝܟ ܣܘܠܩܐ ܕܢܘܗܪܐ ܩܡ

[2] If this is, indeed, the manuscript referred to, I cannot reconcile the measurements.

Syr 4 [formerly: Houghton Syr 4, access *42M-753; Cl 10]

THE NEW TESTAMENT IN THE PESHITTA RECENSION; 1511 Sel at the monastery of Rabban Sabrisho in the Qardo mountains;[1] Estrangelo; partly Nestorian vocal; 332 fol; 27 × 18 cm; vellum; complete; old Oriental wood and leather binding; some coloured geometrical illuminations;[2] A B C F M; according to accompanying note "found in an ancient church in the Assyrian mountains" and handed to Dr. A. Grant by the Nestorian Patriarch Mar Shimon.

Details: Mark 43*b;* Luke 72*a;* John 120*a;* Acts 151*b;* James 200*a;* Hebrews 312*b;* some marginal notes.

[1] I have not checked traditions for proper names. In general, references to details easily ascertainable through an index — such as Catalogue B.M. p. 1136, in this case — are not given. Oddly enough, I see that I stumbled over this name in my first encounter with collections of Syriac manuscripts; cf. *Bulletin of the John Rylands Library* 37 (1955) 434. Cf. Fiey, *Assyrie Chrétienne* (1968) *s.v.*
[2] Cf. Introduction, no. 15.

Syr 5 [formerly: Houghton Syr 5, access *42M-1690; Cl 11, PM p. 54]

LITURGICAL PSALTER:[1,2] 16–17 cent; Nestorian; vocal; 165 fol (damaged in end); 22 × 16 cm; paper; incomplete; A B C F M; obtained from area of Urmia in 1831; similar to MS Syr 3.

[1] No clear terminological differentiation has been established to distinguish a "Book of Psalms", without additions, from a volume clearly marked for liturgical use. A "liturgical Psalter" may add as little as the "Odes" or some indications for worship or it may be arranged for responsive reading, refrains of blessings, etc. and contain also additional hymns, prayers, homilies etc. by Church Fathers. In addition, comments and introductions by the early exegetes — like Theodore of Mopsuestia — may be included. For our descriptions the term will be reserved for this latter type which, of course, is subject to variations, as can be seen from descriptions such as Cat. Cambr. Add 1166 (p. 3). The present volume bears the title: ܓܐ ܟܠܗ ܟܬܒܐܕܗ ܡܟܠܐ ܟܘ̈ܫܐ ܟܠܠܐ ܙܘܐܡ ܟܙܩܐܟ̣ܗ ܡܗܖ̈ܘܐ ܟܒ̇ܐ ܟܐܟ ،ܗ̇ܠ ܕ̣ܙܟ̈ܐܗ ܟܐܩܢܐ ...ܟܘܪܐܘ ܥܘ̇ܐܐܗܪܐ ،ܗ̇ܠ ܕ̣ܙܟ̈ܐܗ ܟܠܠܠܐ ܟܢܠܐܕܐ
I had opted for the term and was confirmed in my choice when I found a description prepared by Baumstark for Katalog Hiersemann 500 (1922) for the manuscript which is now Leiden Or 14.237 (Hebr. 274). To be sure, specialists in liturgy will be able to identify the rite in accordance with the choice of Odes and rubrics, the position of Macarisms, etc. Note, e.g., Cat. Oxford p. 54. Unless otherwise specified, Psalters are in the Peshitta recension.
[2] I do not understand the correction made by Clemons p. 517: "Old Testament ..."

Syr 6 [formerly: Houghton Syr 6, access *42M-1772; Cl 12]

'ABD-ĪŠŌ' BAR BERIKHĀ'S CATALOGUE-POEM ON BOOKS AND WRITERS;[1] 19 cent; Nestorian; partly vocal; 21 fol; 19 × 11 cm; paper; complete; A B C F M; cf. MS Syr 52.

[1] Quoted often since Assemani as Carmen Ebedjesu.

Syr 7 [formerly: Houghton Syr 7, access *42M-1861]

GENESIS I–II IN THE MODERN SYRIAC DIALECT OF ZAKHO; 19 cent; Serto; mixed vocal; 4 fol; 21 × 14 cm; paper; A B C F M.

Details: According to an appended note by one of the missionaries in contact with the A B C F M (Laurie?) this sample was written down in Mosul by a Jacobite "from the lips of a Jew." Dialectological analysis seems of interest. In MS Syr 8, which has had a similar history, a certain Shammas Micha is mentioned; Cf. MS Syr 11.

Syr 8 [formerly: Houghton Syr 8, access *42M-1862]

MATTHEW V–VI IN THE MODERN SYRIAC DIALECT OF ZAKHO; 19 cent; Serto; mixed vocal; 4 fol; 21 × 14 cm; paper; A B C F M; cf. MS Syr 7.

Syr 9 [formerly: Houghton Syr 9, access *42M-1866]

FOUR THEOLOGICAL TRACTS, TRANSLATED FROM MODERN SYRIAC; 19 cent; Nestorian; vocal; 81 (+ 9) fol; 19 × 12 cm; paper; A B C F M.

Details: According to information appended, these tracts had been published in Modern Syriac and then rendered into Classical Syriac by a certain Deacon Joseph. The volume was presented in 1844 by William R. Stocking of Urmia to A B C

F M. The tracts deal with such issues as True Repentance, Faith, Rebirth and ... Satiety and lust for wine.[1]

[1] This tract is termed ܪ̈ܬܡܝܐ ܪܬܐܘܝܐܘ ܪܬܐܘܪ̈. The study of such "inner-Syriac" translations is obviously of linguistic interest. Therefore I note that I discovered the source of the tract against drinking in a small volume which has no title in a European language. This volume — which may not be extant in many copies — was presented by A B C F M to the Andover Theological Seminary, access 51,000, now kept in a special box at Andover-Harvard. The printed volume bears the title ܪ̈ܬܡܝܐ ܪܬܐܩܡܐܘܪܙܐܘ ܪܬܐܘܪ̈.

Syr 10 [formerly: Houghton Syr 10, access *42M-1884; Cl 13]

BOOK OF PRAYERS FOR THE STUDENTS;[1] 19 cent; Nestorian; vocal; 14 fol; 24 × 17 cm; paper; complete; A B C F M.

Details: The collection contains i.a. the Lord's Prayer, the Ten Commandments; Commandments from the Gospels and St. Paul; language mixed quasi-classical and modern Syriac.

[1] I am not sure that ܪ̈ܠܐܩܐܘܪ̈ܬ ܪܬܐܠ̈ does signify this; but it does not look like a "normal" prayer book.

Syr 11 [formerly: Houghton Syr 11, access *42M-1883; Cl 14]

PART OF TRACT ON PROTESTANT ANTI-CATHOLIC DOGMATIC POSITIONS;[1] 19 cent; Serto; partly Nestorian vocal; 20 fol; 23 × 16 cm; paper; beginning missing; A B C F M.

Details: Probably same provenance as MS Syr 7, 8; in the note Micha is mentioned as translator.

[1] The description fol 20a is hardly to be taken as a formal title: ܝܪ̈ܐܬܐ ܪ̈ܩܝܬ ܠ̈ܩܩܠ ܪ̈ܐܝ̈ܠܠ̈ܩܐܬ̈ܐܬ ܪ̈ܩܝܬ An accompanying note uses the term "Protestants' Remembrances".

Syr 12 [formerly: Houghton Syr 12, access *42M-1699F; Cl 15]

BOOK OF SERVICES AND PRAYERS (ḤUDRA): ca 17 cent; Nestorian; partly vocal; 535 fol; 33 × 22 cm; paper; incomplete; old Oriental loose wood and paper binding; A B C F M.

Details: According to note on fly-leaf presented by Mar Yohannan to Dr. Perkins — hence the description as "Mar Yohannan's prayerbook."[1] Dr. Perkins handed the volume to A B C F M in 1858. For the position of this volume cf. the recent bibliography of W.F. Macomber, "A list of the known manuscripts of the Chaldean Ḥudra," *Or Chr Per* 36 (1970) 130.

[1] It stands to reason to suggest that this is the same source from which Perkins got the MS of the *Beth Mawtᵉbhe,* now kept as MS AOS Rn B47B, at Yale-Beinecke.

Syr 13 [formerly: Houghton Syr 13, access *42M-1865]

GENESIS I–VIII IN MODERN SYRIAC; 19 cent; Nestorian; vocal; 10 fol; 28 × 20 cm; paper; complete; A B C F M.

Details: An accompanying note states that the manuscript was written by the priest Ruel Urmanish.[1]

[1] It stands to reason that this is a standardized form and that the said priest was the scribe — in fact, he wrote an accomplished Nestorian hand. The heading states ܐܝܬܘܪܐ ܠܟ ܒܩܒܪܩܐ ܕܝܠ ; but only a special study will identify types of semi-standardized dialectal or supra-dialectal crystallizations.

Syr 14 [formerly: Houghton Syr 14, access *55M-278; SMH 2, access 3945; Ti p. 23; Cl 52][1]

THE NEW TESTAMENT IN THE PESHITTA RECENSION, WITH HARKLEAN PASSION HARMONY;[2] Elul 1521 Sel; Serto; partly vocal; 2 col; 258 fol; 23 × 16 cm; vellum; complete.

Details: Matthew 10*b*; Mark 42*b*; Luke 63*a*; John 99*b*; Acts 138*b*; James 176*a*; Hebrews 247*b*; preceded by prayer (later hand) and table of lessons (3*b*); Harklean passion harmony 128*a*–138*b*; rubricated indication of lessons; written in the monastery of Mar Abraham and Mar Maron in the district of Amida; cf. MS Syr 15.

[1] This is the first among the manuscripts which were transferred from the Semitic Museum to the Houghton library, as indicated in the introduction. This took place in 1955, as indicated by the Houghton accession number. It seems, however, that what happened in 1955 was some kind of finalization of the transfer, and the manuscripts were taken to be kept in Houghton in 1944. This transfer concerns the volumes which are now numbered MS Syr 14–22. These received a label "Harvard College Library" and carried two accession numbers — Semitic Museum and Houghton. It is obvious that this was the beginning of the Harris collection which had come to the Semitic Museum, as indicated by the notation for S M H (there exists no S M H 1).

[2] Some idea as to the widespread use of these texts can be formed from the list in *GSL* p. 188, and much can be added since. A comparison with a codex such as B M Add 18714 *e.g.* shows, however, that the subject of such texts and their use need further inquiry. Note also the remark of S.E. Assemani *ap* J. White, *Sacrorum Evangeliorum Versio Syriaca Philoxeniana* (1778) p. 645. The relevant heading in our codex is ܗ ܐܪܝܡܝܕ ....ܐܩܘܩܬܐ ܐܝܗܕ ܐܬܠܬ ܐܘܠܛܘܐܕ ܐܠܠܛܘܐ ܕ̄ ܐܢܚܢ ܐܝܐܠܝܘܐܘ ܗܘܕܝܕ̄ܪ

Syr 15 [formerly: Houghton Syr 15, access *55M-279; SMH 94, access 4029; Ti p. 201; Cl 132]

THE NEW TESTAMENT IN THE PESHITTA RECENSION, WITH HARKLEAN PASSION HARMONY: ca 12 cent; cursive Estrangelo; 2 col; 206 fol; 22 × 15 cm; vellum; incomplete.

Details: Starting Matthew 21:26; Luke 9*a*; John 38*b*; Acts 72*b*; James 110*b*; Hebrews 197*a*; Harklean passion harmony 64*b*–72*b*.

Syr 16   [formerly: Houghton Syr 16, access *55M-280; SMH
              13, access 3951; Ti p. 28; Cl 58]

THE GOSPELS OF MATTHEW AND MARK IN THE HARKLEAN
RECENSION: 8–9 cent; Estrangelo (two hands?); 63 fol; 25 × 17
cm; vellum; incomplete.

Details: Starting Matthew 8:12; Mark 44*b;* canons, index
sections etc. indicated and summarized for Matthew on fol
42*b;* lessons marked in cursive Estrangelo of the 12th cent;
one of the earliest witnesses of this recension.

Syr 17   [formerly: Houghton Syr 17, access *55M-281; SMH
              117, access 4052; Ti p. 244; Cl 153]

GOSPEL LECTIONARY IN THE HARKLEAN RECENSION:[1] Ḥziran
Sel 1902; semi-professional small Serto; occasional mixed
vocal; 219 fol; 13 × 8 cm; paper; complete.

Details: Detailed colophon; written in the *Qaṣṭra* mountains, in
the monastery of the Virgin and Mar Zakay (?)[2]

[1]   A superficial examination of catalogues reveals different terms,
which may be connected to various rites. This codex is termed ܐܝܢܐ
ܐܒܝܢܐ ܐܬ̇ܩܘ ܡܠܠ ܩܘܠܝܘܐܝܬ̇ܝ̇ܠܝܢ ܐܝܪܘ
[2]   For a monastery named after Mar Zakay cf. *Orient Christ Per*
1977, p. 161. But the identification is far from certain.

Syr 18   [formerly: Houghton Syr 18, access *55M-282; SMH
              53; access 3991; Ti p. 118; Cl 98]

DAMAGED FRAGMENT OF MATTHEW VII–IX IN THE HARKLEAN
RECENSION; ca 10 cent; large Estrangelo; 2 col; 4 fol; 42 × 31
cm; vellum.

Details: Some textual markings, lectionary indications, Syriac
and Greek readings (partly later).

44

Syr 19   [formerly: Houghton Syr 19, access *55M-283; SMH 17, access 3955; Ti p. 30; Cl 62]

FRAGMENT OF GOSPEL LECTIONARY IN THE HARKLEAN RECENSION; ca 10 cent; monumental Estrangelo; occasional Western vocal; 2 col; 1 double fol (external); 42 × 32 cm; vellum; colored ornamental lesson heading.

Details: Parts of John XI–XII, Luke XIX.

Syr 20   [formerly: Houghton Syr 20, access *55M-284; SMH 16, access 3954; Ti p. 30; Cl 61]

FRAGMENT OF GOSPEL LECTIONARY IN THE HARKLEAN RECENSION; 11–12 cent; monumental Estrangelo; 2 col; 1 fol; 45 × 33 cm; vellum; elaborate colored ornamental heading and quire numbering; occasional marginal notations.

Details: Lesson for Palm Sunday — Mark XI; later Syriac and Arabic scribbles.

Syr 21   [formerly: Houghton Syr 21, access *55M-287; SMH 114, access 4049; Ti p. 242; Cl 151; PM p. 54]

PSALTER; 1888 Sel; minute Serto; partly mixed vocal; 147 fol; 5 × 4 cm; paper; complete; original Oriental binding.

Details: Some leaves missing or misplaced; written in Aleppo.

Syr 22   [formerly: Houghton Syr 22, access *55M-288; SMH 50, access 3988; Ti p. 110; Cl 95]

FRAGMENTS OF A COLLECTION OF ECCLESIASTICAL LETTERS AND TREATISES, MAINLY BY SEVERUS OF ANTIOCH OR ADDRESSED TO HIM; ca 10 cent; cursive Estrangelo; 2 col; 80 fol; 26 × 17 cm; paper; incomplete; some rubricated headings.

45

Details: Mostly loose single leaves (torn out of binding and damaged); identification difficult, but it seems that not all the letters are included in the published edition of Brooks *e.a.* (for details cf. Moss, *SPB* 309, 995); other authors of letters include: Thomas, bishop of Germanica to Presbyter John in the monastery of Mar Eusebius in ... Apameia — 15*a;* John Grammaticus Philoponos — 31*b;* Athanasius of Alexandria — 60*b;* probably John Chrysostom — 3*a.*

Syr 23 [formerly: SMH 3, access 3946; Ti p. 24; Cl 53][1]

THE NEW TESTAMENT IN THE PESHITTA RECENSION; 12–13 cent; Serto; occasional vocal; 2 col; 226 (+6) fol; 22 × 15 cm; vellum; incomplete.

Details: Starting Matthew 20:21; Mark 14*a;* Luke 36*b;* John 75*a;* Acts 105*b;* James 145*b;* Hebrews 230*a* (until 5:11); headings of books in Estrangelo; lessons indicated; leaves missing or damaged.

[1]   This is the first of the main bulk of manuscripts belonging to the Semitic Museum which were transferred to the Houghton Library in the late fifties. As opposed to the first lot, these codices were not given at the time Houghton numbers. I decided eventually to continue the numbering so that the first manuscript of the SMH order in this lot was numbered Syr 23. Starting with this manuscript, the numbering is continuous, and no references to the pages of Titterton need be mentioned. To be sure, also the Semitic Museum accession numbers are linked to the continuous Harris numbering.

Syr 24 [formerly: SMH 4, access 3947; Cl 54]

FRAGMENT OF MARK IN THE PESHITTA RECENSION; 12 cent; cursive Estrangelo; 2 col; 8 (+20) fol; 23 × 15 cm; vellum.

Details: Mark 1:1–7:34; lessons indicated.

Syr 25   [formerly: SMH 5, access 3948; Cl 55]

THE GOSPELS IN THE PESHITTA RECENSION; ca 13 cent; semi-professional Serto; occasional later vocal; 156 fol; 15 × 10 cm; vellum; incomplete.

Details: Starting Matthew 21:14, Mark 22*b;* Luke 61*a;* John 126*a* (until 13:32); lessons partly indicated; partly damaged.

Syr 26   [formerly: SMH 6, access 3949; Cl 56]

THE GOSPELS IN THE PESHITTA RECENSION; 1519 Sel; cursive Estrangelo; occasional Western vocal; 158 fol; 15 × 10 cm; vellum; incomplete; some geometrical ornamentation.

Details: Starting Mark 4:4; Luke 39*a;* John 104*b;* lessons and some sections indicated; detailed colophon, hardly legible; partly damaged.

Syr 27   [formerly: SMH 7, access 3950; Cl 57]

THE NEW TESTAMENT IN THE PESHITTA RECENSION; Kanun II 1587 Sel; Nestorian Estrangelo; partly vocal; 227 fol; 19 × 13 cm; paper; some leaves missing.

Details: Starting Matthew 8:21; Mark 28*a;* Luke 49*a;* John 84*a;* Acts 110*b;* James 144*b;* Hebrews 221*a;* sections indicated; detailed colophon.

Syr 28   [formerly: SMH 14, access 3952; Cl 59; Go *Textus* 2 (1962) 52][1]

FRAGMENT OF EZEKIEL XXXIX IN THE SYROHEXAPLA RECENSION:[2] ca 9 cent; Estrangelo; 1 fol; 27 × 18 cm; vellum.

Details: Text 39:8–17; some marginal readings from the "Three"; partly faded.[3]

[1] Note the later inventories of Syrohexaplaric materials in W. Baars *New Syro-Hexaplaric Texts* (1968); A. Vööbus, *The Hexapla and the Syro-Hexapla* (1971); cf. also his *Discoveries of very important sources for the Syro-Hexapla* (1970).

[2] This fragment does not come, as far as I can compare, from the codex to which B M Add 14668 fol 26 f. belonged. The lines in the Harvard MS are 21/23.

[3] In light of the textual exercise carried out in the article mentioned Introduction, above n. 1, the almost complete textual identity between this fragment and the Milano MS ought to be stressed. Still, this leaf shows one real scribal mishap (ܪܥܠܘܫ for ܪܡܝܘܫ in v. 13) and one omission of a marginal variant. To the scribal variations noted by Baars p. 13, one should add in v. 16 ܡܠܝܘܒܩ for ܡܝܘܒܩ in the Milano MS.

Syr 29 [formerly: SMH 15, access 3953; Cl 60]

DAMAGED FRAGMENT OF GOSPEL LECTIONARY IN THE PESHITTA RECENSION, CONTAINING PARTS OF MATTHEW IX, XI, XII; ca 12 cent; Estrangelo; 2 col; 1 double fol; 31 × 21 cm; vellum.

Details: Lessons rubricated in text, partly added later.

Syr 30 [formerly: SMH 18, access 3956; Cl 63]

BOOK OF SERVICES AND PRAYERS: ORDERS FOR THE YEAR: ca 12 cent; cursive Estrangelo; occasional vocal; 2 col; 312 fol; 45 × 33 cm; vellum; incomplete.

Details: Many hymns ascribed to Aphrem or Jacob of Serug; some notes in later Serto; similarity to MS Syr 102 to be checked; severely damaged in beginning.

48

Syr 31 [formerly: SMH 19, access 3957: Cl 64]

BOOK OF SERVICES AND PRAYERS: ORDERS AND COMMEMORA-
TIONS FOR THE YEAR (FESTIVALS); ca 12 cent; cursive Estrangelo (different hands); rare Western vocal; 2 col; 205 fol;
45 × 34 cm; vellum; incomplete; some illuminations (cf. 116*b*).

Details: Many hymns ascribed to Aphrem or Jacob of Serug;[1]
signature of scribe 196*b*;[2] owner's note (?) 1*a*; partly damaged.

[2] He signs as deacon ܫܡܘܢ, but it is difficult to make out the letters.

Syr 32 [formerly: SMH 20, access 3958; Cl 65]

SEVERELY DAMAGED FRAGMENTS OF A VOLUME OF HOMILIES
(MĒMRĒ) BY JACOB OF SERUG BOUND TOGETHER WITH TWO
SLIGHTLY LATER FRAGMENTARY LEAVES FROM A BOOK OF
SERVICES; 11 cent; cursive Estrangelo; 2 col; 11 fol; original
size ca 41 × 29 cm; vellum.

Details: According to partly illegible heading 9*b* possibly
arranged for the passion week; contains parts of homilies on
paralytic, blind man and son of the widow.

Syr 33 [formerly: SMH 21, access 3959; Cl 66]

FRAGMENT OF A COMMENTARY ON PASSAGES FROM JEREMIAH
VI-IL;[1] 19 cent; Serto; partly Nestorian vocal; 10 fol; 36 × 25
cm; paper.

[1] Sample for identification from beginning of fragment (6:29): ܬܪܝܢ
At the end a pencilled note to Harris, written in Syriac.

49

Syr 34 [formerly SMH 22, access 3960; Cl 67]

FRAGMENT FROM AN ECCLESIASTICAL HISTORY (?), DEALING WITH A STATEMENT OF FAITH, THE MIRACULOUS ESCAPE OF ATHANASIUS,[1] ETC; ca 12 cent; cursive Estrangelo; 3 col; one damaged fol; ca 30 × 21 cm; vellum.

[1] The following may serve as sample for identification:
ܘܦܩܕ ܡܠܟܐ ܢܘܗܪܐ ܕܬܘܕܝܬܐ ܟܠܗܘܢ ܐܢܫܝܢ ܕܡܗܝܡܢܝܢ ܒܡܠܬܐ ܕܟܢ
ܐܢܬܘܬܐ ܗܘ. ܥܠ ܐܬܢܐܣܝܘܣ ܕܝܢ ܦܩܕ ܕܟܠ ܐܢܫ ܕܢܫܟܚܝܘܗܝ ܒܬܫܟܚܬܗ(?) ܢܩܛܘܠ
Not enough details remain to identify Athanasius.

Syr 35 [formerly: SMH 23, access 3961; Cl 68]

HISTORY OF THE VIRGIN;[1] 16–17 cent; inelegant Serto; 148 fol; 18 × 13 cm; paper; incomplete; some leaves misplaced.

Details: Subdivided into six books; 135*b* starts a homily on Mary and Joseph[2] attributed to Aphrem.[3]

[1] ܟܬܒܐ ܕܬܫ̈ܥܝܬܐ ܕܝܠܕܬ ܐܠܗܐ ܡܪܝܡ
[2] ܥܠ ܡܪܝܡ ܘܝܘܣܦ ܘܥܠ ܚܫܕ[ܐ] ܕܚܫܕܘܗ ܡܢ ܒܢܝ̈ܢܫܐ ܠܛܘܒܢܝܬܐ
[3] From a comparison of a fair number of manuscripts of this type it would seem that this homily was generally said to be "in the meter of Aphrem"; cf. MS Syr 36.

Syr 36 [formerly: SMH 24, access 3962; Cl 69]

A COLLECTION OF MIRACLE STORIES, HISTORY OF THE VIRGIN AND RELATED HOMILIES; 16–17 cent (different hands); semi-professional Serto; 117 fol; 21 × 15 cm; paper; incomplete; partly damaged and out of sequence.

Details: Fragments from the miracle story of Bar Ṣauma of Nisibis (cf. Baumstark, *GSL* p. 180) fol 1 f, 82 f; parts of Books 5 and 6 of the *History of the Virgin* (fol 12 f; end indicated fol 61*a*); homilies and stories on the Virgin, among them as noted for MS Syr 35 and one attributed to Jacob of Serug (fol 61*b* f); also one leaf (fol 11) from lectionary containing parts of I Thess IV and John V in the Peshitta recension.

Syr 37 [formerly: SMH 25, access 3963; Cl 70]

BAR HEBRAEUS: THE BOOK OF RAYS; 15 cent; Serto; partly mixed vocal; 302 fol; 18 × 12 cm; vellum (paper after fol 239 and some leaves in between); complete; Oriental wood binding.

Details: A considerable part of the MS is palimpsest, written over an 11 cent cursive Estrangelo 2 col text of homilies, some of which are suggestive of Aphrem's style and worth deciphering; the colophon has been tampered with, but Kanun I 1866 Sel seems possible.

Syr 38 [formerly: SMH 26, access 3964; Cl 71]

A COLLECTION OF RELIGIOUS (EDIFYING) STORIES AND TRACTS: 15–16 cent; Serto (different hands); second hand occasional Western vocal; 236 fol; 18 × 13 cm; paper; incomplete; Oriental wood-leather binding.

Details: Story of Mar Cyriacus (fol 1*a;* subscription 49*b*[1]); letters from Heaven (fol 49*b*);[2] story of Mar Shalita (fol 83*a* — beginning of different hand);[3] wonderdeed[4] of Philoxenus of Mabbug (fol 111*b*); abbreviated story of the Apostle Thomas (fol 122*a*); short tracts on holy men (Mar John from Dailan in Persia; Eulogius;[5] Mar John from Kaphane, etc.).

---

[1] ܩܘܢܝܛܘܣ ܝܢ‌....ܗ ܟ‌ܘܗ ܟܕ‌ܝ‌ܫܬ. For the analysis of the story by Dillmann cf. Moss, *SPB s.v.* The version in Bedjan *Acta Martyrum* III ought to be compared.

[2] Cf. the remarks in Assemani — *Bib Or* III, I p. 638 and Bittner,

Denkschriften kais. Akademie Wien, phil-hist Cl. 51 (1906) 92 f; for different types note Mingana's *Catalogue* I s.v. letter and see Ebied, *Or. Chr. Anal* 197 (1974) 525. It may be worthwhile to remember that Bittner's Syriac material came largely from the three manuscripts belonging to Harris.

[3] Since I cannot compare MS Berlin Syr 176 to BM Add 25875, I must leave open the possibility that there exists a "Shalita-poem" which is not identical with the prose *vita.* It stands to reason that what was MS Urmi 110 has not been saved. Our MS contains a prose *vita,* starting with the fifth chapter (out of seven): ܪܫܐ ܕܫܠܝܛܐ ܥܠ ܡܥܠܬܗ ܕܡܪܝ، ܫܠܝܛܐ ܒܡܡܠܠܐ ܥܡ ܡܪܝ، ܐܘܓܝܢ

By the way, in checking the BM manuscript I looked at the end of the *vita* (ib, fol 253*a*) and was struck by seeing in an 18 cent Nestorian codex what to me looked like a Judeo-Persian hand. Wright's remark (p. 1069) should be adjusted to indicate that the Peshitta of Psalms 22:17–21 appears in untrained Judeo-Persian letters. I would almost suspect a Christian scribe trying his hand; cf. ib fol 362. I leave it to others to follow up the possible implications.

[4] Perhaps "triumph" would render the quality of *neṣḥānā* in this context. The heading suggests that such a collection was prepared for reading on respective memorial days: ܢܨܚܢܐ.... ܕܡܢ ܬܫܥܝܬܗ ܕܩܕܝܫܐ ܡܪܝ، ܐܟܣܢܝܐ.... ܕܕܘܟܪܢܗ ܐܘܟܝܬ ܠܥܘܢܕܢܗ ܠܡܩܪܐ ܒܝܘܡ ܥܕܥܕܐ

[5] The relation to the Syro-Palestinian material ought to be checked.

Syr 39 [formerly: SMH 27, access 3965; Cl 72]

THE CAVE OF TREASURES AND THE HISTORY OF THE VIRGIN; Teshrin II 2168 Sel; Serto; partly mixed vocal; 237 (+2) fol; 16 × 11 cm; paper; incomplete.

Details: Detailed Garshuni colophon fol 95*b,* before beginning of the "history"; short note fol 237*a.*

Syr 40 [formerly: SMH 28, access 3966; Cl 73; PM p. 54]

PSALTER AND CANTICLES; Syriac and Garshuni in parallel col; Ḥziran 1870 Sel; Serto; vocal and spirant; 249 fol; 20 × 14 cm; paper; complete (some leaves repaired).

Details: Psalm 151 and Canticles 228a; Nicene creed and discourse on love of learning 241b; detailed colophon 227b; 229a.

Syr 41 [formerly: SMH 29, access 3967; Cl 74]

A COLLECTION OF COMMENTARIES, TRACTS AND HOMILIES, MAINLY BY MOSES BAR KEPHA;[1] 2121 Sel; Serto; occasional mixed vocal; 246 (+3) fol; 22 × 16 cm; paper; complete; some colored geometrical illuminations.

Details: Commentary on Gospel of John 3b; tracts on lexicographical, grammatical and exegetical points attributed to Bar Kepha 9b; homilies, partly divided into sub-arrangements 11a.[2] Short exegetical notes (*nuhārē*) 230a.[3] The volume also contains short tracts by other authors, such as Jacob of Edessa on "Beginnings of this type of monasticism"; homily by Jacob of Serug 220b; inventory of patriarchal life spans by George of the Gentiles[4] 240a; Apocalypse of Macarius 241b;[5] poem in Persian "Garshuni" 245b.

---

[1] The name appears in various forms, often as ܐܡܝܢ ܪܝܫܩܘܦܐ ܗܘ ܐܦܪܐ ܬܒ ܠܬܐܕܗܝܬ ܐܡ ܟܐܦܐ The present volume, as well as MS Syr 112 may add to the observations on the *oevre* of Bar Kepha made by Vööbus, *Abr-Nahrain* 10 (1970) 123 f.; *HTR* 68 (1975) 377 f.; and by Schlimme in *A Tribute to Arthur Vööbus* (ed. Robert H. Fischer), Chicago 1977, 332 f.
[2] Festal homilies end 192a with the subscription ܫܠܡ.... ܟܬܒܐ ܕܚܫܐ ܟܐܦܐ ܬܒ ....ܡܪܝ ܕܝܪܝܐ ܕܡܬ; cf. the subscription MS B. M. Add 21210 fol 132a; cf. Baumstark, *GSL* p. 282.
[3] Probably also by Bar Kepha, but in need of identification.
[4] Known also by the title "Bishop of the Arabs."
[5] Note the edition by A. van Lantschoot, *Muséon* 63 (1950) 168 f; cf. MS Syr 59.

Syr 42 [formerly: SMH 30, access 3968; Cl 75]

THEOLOGICAL TRACTS AND EPISTLES, MAINLY BY JOHN OF DALYATHA ('JOHN SABA') AND JOHN BAR PENKAYE[1]; 16–17 cent; inelegant Serto; mainly 2 col; 125 fol; 26 × 18 cm; paper; incomplete; cf. MS Syr 115.

Details: Discourse on monastic life by John of Dalyatha 1*a;* fifty-one epistles by him 33*a;* discourses on knowledge by Bar Penkaye 67*a;* various epistles and hymns 93*b;* metrical discourses of Bar Penkaye 98*a; neshānā*[2] of Bar Penkaye 101*b;* homilies by Evagrius (102*b*), Gregory the Monk (109*a*), Simon the Monk *(ib),* Basilius (111*b*), Philoxenus (112*b*), Chrysostom (114*b*); Apocalypse of Daniel 117*a;* some further discourses 122*b*.[3]

[1] A subscription fol 97*b* has been copied from a *Vorlage* which contained at least (?) the writings by John Saba. I cannot find the basis for the form used by Moss, *SPB* 564: John *Bar* D. Cf. note on MS Syr 115.
[2] Cf. note on MS Syr 38.
[3] The author of the first of these is called ܝܘܚܢܢ ܕܩܠܝܡ ܣܘܣ. I cannot check at present whether this is, indeed, John Climax (who apparently keeps the Greek form of his name, or its abbreviation).

Syr 43 [formerly: SMH 31, access 3969; Cl 76]

FRAGMENTS FROM A COLLECTION OF ACTS OF THE SAINTS AND RELATED ORDERS; ca 17 cent; inelegant Serto; 18 fol; 26 × 17 cm; paper; incomplete.

Details: From the story of Cyriacus and Julitta 1*a;*[1] order for Shamuni;[2] mixed fragments from the story of Malka[3] of Clysma and Mar John 11*a.*

[1] It will need further comparison to establish possible identities or differences between "stories," "commemorations," or "acts" connected with a certain saint. Different terms like ܩܠܐ, ܕܘܟܪܢܐ, ܬܫܥܝܬܐ may

54

refer to the same literary creation. Cf. Bedjan, *Acta martyrum et sanctorum* III (1892) 254 and Mingana No. 542.

[2] ܪܝܒܠܗ ܕ؛ܐܝܟܐ ܡܝܝܒܐ ܙܒܨܝ ܒܝ̣ܒ ܠܝ̄ܝ ܪܡܒܠ

[3] I have used this name as spelled in Sachau's index with misgivings. I suspect it is rather "Malkē" (*malki*), for the manuscript uses *seyāmē*, which fits Bedjan, *Acta* V p. 422.

Syr 44 [formerly: SMH 32, access 3970; Cl 77]

ORDER FOR MATRIMONIAL SERVICES (PARTLY GARSHUNI) AND ORDER OF THE VIRGIN FOR IYAR;[1] 1829 Sel (different hands); semi-professional Serto; partly vocal and spirant; 31 fol; 26 × 16 cm; paper; incomplete.

Details: Order for the Virgin 23*b*.

[1] The heading describes one of the Orders as ܪܟܚܘܼ ܝ̄ܝܩܗ ܪܡܒܠ ܪܕܠܠܗܐ. The colophon fol 22*a* describes as follows: ܪܬܒܟ̈ܗ ܪܟܚܐ ܪܘܩܝܩܒܐ ܪܝܡܐܟܝ ܪܟܝܩܒܗܐ ܪܘܝܪ̈ܒܝ ܪ̈ܝܪܟܗ ܪܘܝܐ̈ܝܩܐ ܪܕܐ[ܒܝ]ܒ̈ܝܗܐ ܪܠܙ̈ܝܗ ʼܐܕܠܪܝ ܪܘܝܪ ؛ܝܪܗ ܡܐܒܗܗ …. ܦܬܝ̈ܝ ܪܡܐܝܪ ܕܝܬܠܗ ܪ̈ܝܪܟܗ ܪܡܒܠ؛ܒܐ I must leave it to specialists in liturgical matters to explain why all these go together.

Syr 45 [formerly: SMH 33, access 3971; Cl 78]

SELECTIONS FROM THE DIDASCALIA APOSTOLORUM, THE EPISTLES OF IGNATIUS OF ANTIOCH AND FROM CYRIL'S COMMENTARY; Tamuz 2207 Sel: Serto; 19 fol; 27 × 20 cm; paper; incomplete.

Details: Part of a larger volume, original numeration starting as p. 79; only one side of each leaf used, and some details entered by Harris; copy possibly prepared for him in connection with his projects; selections from Ignatius p. 95; Cyril's commentary on Jesus' baptism (from Luke) p. 103.[1]

[1] Cf. Chabot, *Corpus Scriptorum Chr. Or, Scr. Syri* IV, I (1912) 23 f; the recent article by J.M. Sauget, "Nouvelles homilies du Commentaire sur l'Evangile de S. Luc de Cyrille d'Alexandrie," *Or. Chr. An.* 197 (1974) 439 f. does not deal with this part.

Syr 46 [formerly: SMH 34, access 3972; Cl 79]

FRAGMENTS OF THE DISCOURSES OF GREGORY NAZIANZEN: ca 10 cent; Estrangelo; occasional Western vocal; 2 col; 12 fol; 26 × 19 cm; vellum; rubricated headings and subscriptions.

Details: fol 1*a* contains end of index, mentioning sections 44–47; parts from discourse on moderation in speech (No. 31) 1*b* and on dogma and constitution of bishops 8*b*.[1]

[1] A preliminary comparison suggests that our text goes together with B. M. Add 14549 not with Add 17146. The terms are ܐܪܝܘܬ ܕܡܠܠܘܬܐ and ܕܥܠ ܩܢܘܢܐ ܘܛܟܣܐ ܕܐܦܣܩܘܦܐ ܕܡܠܠܘܬܐ.

Syr 47 [formerly: SMH 35, access 3973; Cl 80]

A VOLUME OF THEOLOGICAL TRACTS, HOMILIES AND SCHOLIA MAINLY BY JOHN OF DARA, MOSES BAR KEPHA, CYRIL, JACOB OF EDESSA, SEVERUS OF ANTIOCH, DIONYSIUS BAR ṢALIBI; ca 16 cent; Serto (different hands); 2 col; 207 fol; 26 × 16 cm; paper; incomplete; partly damaged by water; partly Oriental wood binding.

Details: Parts of discourses 4–10 on the soul by John of Dara[1] 4*a*; related discourses on the soul and on resurrection, mainly by John the Stylite from Yathrib (53*a*) and Moses Bar Kepha (64*a*);[2] excerpts from discourses by Jacob of Serug, Cyril, John of Dara, Phyloxenus etc. 105*b*; excerpts and summaries from Cyril's *Glaphyra* on Genesis — from the story of Cain to the sale of Joseph 120*b*; exegetical notes of Hippolyte on Jacob's blessing of Judah, on quails and manna 137*a*; notes from Jacob of Edessa 140*b*; excerpts from the Epithronia (Cathedral homilies) of Severus of Antioch 151*a*; exegetical "arguments"[4] by Xystus of 'Rome 158*a*; excerpts from Isidore (of Pelusium?)[5] 158*b*; canons on the Order of the Holy Mysteries by Mar John (?) 161*a*; scholia by Jacob of Edessa on the Eucharist 162*a;* tracts on faith, baptism, olive oil, holy chrism by Dionysius Bar Salibi 163*b;* further tracts on these subjects 168*b.*

[1] I have normalized "John," although this author is among those who are known by the Greek form of the name, "Iwannis." For this author cf. the introduction to the recent edition of his *de oblatione* by J. Sader, *CSCO* 132 (Louvain 1970). The discourses in this MS are from his ܪ̈ܥܐ ܠܒܕ ܐܟܪ̈ܬܐ; see subscription 52*b.*
[2] Cf. for these MS Syr 112.
[3] As far as I can see this was not used for the edition of *Les Homiliae Cathedrales de Sévère d'Antioche,* begun by M. Brière and continued by F. Graffin and C. Lash; cf. *Patrologia Orientalis* 29 (1960); 35 (1969) ff.
[4] The exact nuances of terminology remain to be studied; these are ܪܚ̣ܘܬܐ.
[5] This seems to be the reference intended by ܕܡܪ̈ܝ ܐ̈ܠܡܠܐ.

Syr 48 [formerly: SMH 36, access 3974; Cl 81]

A VOLUME OF THEOLOGICAL ("ASCETIC") TRACTS; 2108 Sel (see fol 295*a*); Serto; partly Nestorian vocal; 297 fol; 23 × 16 cm; paper; complete.

Details: Monastic rules 1*b;* excerpts from Philoxenus, Basilius, Isaiah of Scete, Chrysostom; Evagrius, John of Dalyatha 3*b;* epistles by Jacob of Serug and Nilus 42*b;* homilies by Isaac (of Nineve?) 51*b;* extracts from epistles and homilies of some Fathers 54*a;* Isaiah of Scete on "impassibility"[1] 77*b;* eight discourses of Isaac of Antioch 81*a;* Jacob of Serug on monks 101*a;* the third part of Palladius' *Paradise* 111*a;* Addenda 295*b.*

[1] Cf. which terms Smith's *Thesaurus* notes as being rendered by ܪܠ ܪܚܐܙܐܘ.

57

Syr 49   [formerly: SMH 37, access 3975; Cl 82]

FUNERAL SERVICES;[1] partly Garshuni; 1980 Sel; occasional mixed vocal; 102 fol; 22 × 14 cm; paper; complete.

Details: Subdivisions according to the Order of Services for clergy (2*b*), laymen (40*b*), women (63*a*), and children (82*a*); some Old Testament lessons are in the Syrohexapla recension[2] and some New Testament lessons in the Harklean; parts of John V in the Harklean recension added by later hand fol 102.

[1]   The terms are ܪܠܐܠܗ ܪܒܟܗ — *kitāb taǧnīz*; cf. the Garshuni fol 54*a*, 74*a*. For publication of some Syrohexapla material from this MS cf. Introduction, above n.1.

[2]   For details cf. the above mentioned article; cf. MS Syr 85, 88.

Syr 50   [formerly: SMH 38, access 3976; Cl 83]

DAMAGED FRAGMENT FROM MARK XII IN THE PESHITTA RECENSION; ca 11 cent; cursive Estrangelo; 1 fol *verso*; 23 × 15 cm; vellum.[1]

[1]   *Recto* contains end of a prayer in later Serto hand and notes in Syriac and Armenian concerning some attack on Christians in Zed (?) in 1310.

Syr 51   [formerly: SMH 39, access 3977; Cl 84]

TWO DAMAGED FRAGMENTS OF STORIES AND PRAYERS; ca 14 cent; inelegant Nestorian; partly vocal; 2 fol; 17 × 11 cm; paper.

Details: One leaf contains parts of the story of Arsenius, king of Egypt; one leaf contains parts of prayer and hymn.[1]

[1]   Harris noted the publication of the Arsenius ("Arsānīs") text by Hall, *Hebraica* 6 (1890) 81 f. Hall did not have this text at his disposal; cf. MS Syr 166.

58

Syr 52 [formerly: SMH 40, access 3978; Cl 85]

A VOLUME OF WRITINGS BY ʿABD-ĪŠŌʿ BAR BERĪKHĀ; Teshrin II 1865 Sel (cf. fol 70*b*);[1] Nestorian; partly vocal; 98 fol; 16 × 10 cm; paper; incomplete; partly Oriental wood binding; cf. MS Syr 66.

Details: The "Pearl" 1*a*; Nestorian credo in Arabic (Syriac heading) 71*b*; the major part of his catalogue poem on books and writers 76*b*.

[1] Since this is one of the older MSS, it may be worthwhile to mention in this case that the MS was written ܠܟܝ .... ܪܟܘܪܬܒܝ ܪܕܬܝܠܒ ܪܠܒܬܐ ܪܝܡܢܝ ܒܠܡܬ ܠܝܟ.

Syr 53 [formerly: SMH 41, access 3979; Cl 86]

POLEMICAL WRITINGS OF DIONYSIUS BAR ṢALIBI; 19 cent; Serto; partly 2 col; 55 fol; 25 × 17 cm; paper; complete.

Details: Discourse against Muslims 1*a*; discourse against Chalcedonians 32*a*.[1]

[1] I am at a loss to understand the remark of Clemons on this MS, the more so since he mentions a doctoral dissertation at an institution with which he was, I think, connected. This MS does not contain the discourse against Jews and it is not cod. Harris 83 (now = MS Syr 91). The mistake may have occurred, because this is one of the MSS kept back by Harris when the collection was shipped to the Semitic Museum. It arrived only in 1906 — the year when deZwaan published his edition of "Bar Ṣalibi against the Jews." The correction in Clemons p. 516 should be quite unqualified.

Syr 54 [formerly: SMH 42, access 3980; Cl 87]

LEXICON OF THE SYRIAC LANGUAGE BY BAR BAHLUL, with admixtures from other lexicographers; Ab 1972 Sel; Serto;

mixed vocal; 2 col; 372 fol; 30 × 20 cm; paper; complete; partly Oriental wood binding.

Details: In this MS Armenian (in Syriac script) has been substituted for the usual Arabic glosses;[1] detailed final colophon and intermediate colophons at the end of each letter, partly Garshuni; Arabic fragments in binding.

[1] Margoliouth, *JRAS* 1898, p. 839 f. has discussed this MS in detail and explored its composite character. It is sometimes quoted in Smith's *Thesaurus.* I cannot recall having seen a Syriac-Armenian dictionary; but the uncatalogued MS Syr Yale 9 seems to contain such a lexicon as well as some glossary list. (The Armenian character needs verification.)

Syr 55 [formerly: SMH 43, access 3981; Cl 88]

MONASTIC HISTORY BY THOMAS OF MARGA;[1] Ab 1888 C.E.; Nestorian; vocal; 201 fol; 33 × 23 cm; paper; complete.

[1] Whereas the colophon uses the title of "Book of Governors," the superscription is descriptive, as in Budge's edition. I have not checked Titterton's statement that the text of this MS is close to that of the edition.

Syr 56 [formerly: SMH 44, access 3982; Cl 89]

THE HEXAEMERON HOMILIES OF EMANUEL BAR SHAHARE;[1] Adar 1881 C.E.; Nestorian; partly vocal; 125 fol; 33 × 21 cm; paper; complete; cf. MS Andover-Harvard 329.

[1] The title is given as ܪܝܫܐܐ ܕܐܘܠܝܬܐ .... ܪܝܫܐ ܕܐܬܥ ܪܒܐ ܕܥܠܡܐ ܕܗܘ ܪܒܐ ܕܥܠ. This MS shares with others the omission of the second homily and the addition of the homily on baptism (fol 123a).

Syr 57 [formerly: SMH 45, access 3983; Cl 90]

FRAGMENTS FROM A COLLECTION OF THEOLOGICAL TREATISES BY ISAAC OF NINEVE; 13–14 cent; cursive-angular Estrangelo; 59 fol; 19 × 13 cm; vellum.

Details: Discourses deal with subjects such as birth of spiritual feeling, contemplation, upbringing of man, etc., which make identification highly likely; mostly rubricated headings for various treatises (discourses); partly considerably damaged.

Syr 58 [formerly: SMH 46, access 3984; Cl 91]

PROLOGUES AND READINGS ACCORDING TO EUTHALIUS ON THE PAULINE EPISTLES; 19 cent; Serto; 39 fol;[1] 27 × 20 cm; paper; complete.

[1] Script on *verso* only. Harris noted that he had this copy prepared from a MS at Deir Zaafran, and he entered certain readings from B. M. Add 7157. The description in RF has to be supplemented, of course, from Wright's catalogue p. 1203. My comparison of the B. M. manuscript and a study of the *incipits* in Mingana 343 *B* suggest that the Syriac text tradition is not quite uniform and ought to be studied.

Syr 59 [formerly: SMH 47, access 3985; Cl 92]

A COLLECTION OF MIRACLE STORIES, 'APOCRYPHAL' WRITINGS AND COMMEMORATIVE READINGS;[1] Tamuz 2168 Sel; Serto; partly mixed vocal and spirant; 240 fol; 23 × 16 cm; paper; complete; partly Oriental wood binding; some colored geometrical illuminations.

Details: Conundrums 5*a;* Apocalypse of Macarius *ib;*[2] miracle stories (partly in meter); among those Ananias and Shamuni, Abba Moses the Black, Sons of Jacob 14*a;* commemorative reading for the feast of Assumption 77*b;* youth and upbringing of Jesus (from History of the Virgin) 86*a;* dialogue between Moses and God on Sinai 105*a;* Apocalypse of Paul[3] 117*a;* parts from the 'Cave of Treasures' 159*b;* further miracle stories and *Sughithas* 203*b.*

[1]   The nature of the volume is summed up in the colophon as ܪܒܬܐ
ܪܟܝܠܝܢܐ ܪܝܢ ܗܝܢܪܬ ܪܬܘܪܟܬ ܪܗܡܩܘܐ ܪܝܢܝܗܢ.
[2]   Cf. MS Syr 41.
[3]   Cf. Riciotti, *Orientalia* 2 (1933) 1 f, 120 f.

Syr 60   [formerly: SMH 48, access 3986; Cl 93]

DAMAGED FRAGMENTS OF TWO POEMS, ONE BY GEORGE WARDA; 17–18 cent; Nestorian; partly vocal; 4 fol; 28 × 20 cm; paper.

Details: One poem with rubricated commentary after each line; poem by Warda on famine, pestilence and drought 3*b.*

Syr 61   [formerly: SMH 49, access 3987; Cl 94]

DAMAGED FRAGMENTS FROM BOOK OF SERVICES AND PRAYERS; 12–13 cent; cursive Estrangelo; 2 col; 8 fol; 45 × 28 cm; vellum.

Details: Occasional later marginal notation in Greek.

Syr 62   [formerly: SMH 51, access 3989;[1] Cl 96]

DAMAGED FRAGMENTS FROM MARK I–II, VII–XIII AND LUKE I IN THE PESHITTA RECENSION; ca 7 cent; Estrangelo; 2 col; 11 fol; 26 × 21 cm; vellum.

Details: Luke I fol 11*a;* some later marginal lectionary notes.

[1]   Whereas the present numbering follows the SMH order, the accession numbering does not always proceed *pari passu.*

62

Syr 63 [formerly: SMH 52, access 3990; Cl 97]

DAMAGED FRAGMENTS FROM MATTHEW XXIV AND JOHN XI–XII IN THE PESHITTA RECENSION; ca 8 cent; Estrangelo; 2 col; 5 fol; 26 × 21 cm; vellum.

Details: John 2*b;* some later marginal lectionary notes.

Syr 64 [formerly: SMH 54, access 3992; Cl 99]

TREASURY OF MYSTERIES — THE SCHOLIA OF BAR HEBRAEUS ON THE BIBLE; 1875 C.E.; Serto; partly mixed vocal; 2 col; 399 fol; 31 × 21 cm; paper; complete;[1] cf. MS Syr 119.

Details: Intermediate colophon after end of O.T., fol 277*a.*

[1] This MS has been discussed by W.C. Graham, *AJSL* 41 (1925) 102 in the context of prestudies towards the Chicago edition.

Syr 65 [formerly: SMH 55, access 3993; Cl 100]

BAR HEBRAEUS: ETHICS; 1894 C.E.; Serto; partly mixed vocal; 2 col; 190 fol; 34 × 24 cm; paper; complete.

Syr 66 [formerly: SMH 56, access 3994; Cl 101]

A VOLUME OF WRITINGS BY 'ABD-ĪŠŌ' BAR BERĪKHĀ; Teshrin I 1892 C.E.;[1] Nestorian; vocal; 116 fol; 33 × 23 cm; paper; complete; cf. MS Syr 52.

Details: Paradise of Eden 1*b;* Pearl 93*b.*

[1] In this instance a note on the fate of a volume may be in order. MSS Syr 66 and 67 were copied in 1892 by the same scribe in Tel Kephe — probably by commission — and they have stayed together. The next year the scribe copied MS Syr 77. But, as stated in the Introduction, we usually cannot go in for this kind of observation. Cf. note on MS Syr 113.

Syr 67   [formerly: SMH 57, access 3995; Cl 102]

ORDER FOR COMMEMORATION AND METRIC LIFE STORY OF RABBAN HORMIZD, THE PERSIAN;[1] Ḥziran 1892 C.E.; Nestorian; vocal; 93 fol; 33 × 23 cm; paper; complete; cf. MS Syr 145; UTS MS Syr 20.

Details: Order 1*b;* metrical life story by Sergius of Azarbeidjan 28*a.*

[1] I have not checked Titterton's statement to the effect that the text is in close agreement with that of the Budge edition.

Syr 68   [formerly: SMH 58, access 3996; Cl 103]

BAR HEBRAEUS: CANDLESTICK OF THE SANCTUARIES — THE COMPENDIUM OF DOGMATICS; Tishrin I 1893 C.E.; Serto; partly mixed vocal; 314 fol (Syriac pagination 623 p.); 33 × 22 cm; paper; complete.

Syr 69   [formerly: SMH 59, access 3997; Cl 104]

BAR HEBRAEUS: NOMOCANON — THE COMPENDIUM OF CANON LAW; Nisan 1895 C.E.; Serto; partly mixed vocal; 2 col; 134 (+5) fol (Syriac pagination 269 p.); 33 × 23 cm; paper; complete.

Syr 70   [formerly: SMH 60, access 3998; Cl 105]

ISHO'DAD OF MERV: COMMENTARY ON ACTS AND EPISTLES; Tishrin I 1893 C.E.; Serto; partly mixed vocal; 2 col; 133 fol; 27 × 19 cm; paper; complete.

Details: Commentary on Epistle of James 32*a.*[1]

[1] This MS is referred to by Harris in his contribution to the Introduction to Mrs. Gibson's edition, *Horae Semiticae* V (1911) XV; cf. MS Syr 131.

64

Syr 71 [formerly: SMH 61, access 3999; Cl 106]

TWENTY SEVEN OF THE DISCOURSES OF ISAAC OF ANTIOCH;[1]
Elul 1895 C.E.; Serto (different hands, partly semi-
professional); partly mixed vocal; 157 (+3) fol (Syriac pagination 315 p.); 23 × 16 cm; paper; complete.

Details: The volume contains perhaps one quarter of the
discourses of the author. As in other cases, the substitution of
Aphrem's name has to be studied. p. 298 starts a homily by
Aphrem on the time of death.[2]

[1] The authorship was clear to Harris. The attribution to Isaac of
Nineve (p. 297 of Syriac pagination) is a lapsus calami.
[2] For the problems cf. Baumstark, *GSL* p. 64.

Syr 72 [formerly: SMH 62, access 4000; Cl 107]

A VOLUME OF EXEGETICAL TREATISES, EXTRACTS AND EPISTLES;
17–18 cent; semi-professional Nestorian (different hands);[1]
partly vocal; 162 fol; 22 × 16 cm; paper; incomplete.

Details: Scholia and explanations of words in the Old Testament (1*a*) and New Testament (17*b*); extracts from Chrysostom, Epiphanius and others 43*b;* questions from the scholia of
Theodore 48*a;*[2] further exegetical extracts 62*b;* lexicographical selections (i.a., from Ḥonain and 'Anan-Īšō') and directions
for correct reading 65*b;* extracts from Īšō' Bar Nūn (85*b*) and
from the canons by Ḥonain and 'Anan-Īšō' 90*a;*[3] extracts from
the questions of Joseph Hazzaya[4] 118*b;* epistles 122*b;* fables by
Aesop 152*a;* sayings of wisdom 161*b.*

[1] There are at least three hands. A change of hand occurs fol 65*b;*
fol 122–136 is written in a somewhat earlier hand. Sequences are
partly disturbed.
[2] The nature of these questions is theological rather than exegetical.
I doubt whether this is what is referred to in the sources adduced by
Baumstark, *GSL* p. 104, n. 8. For a recent summary of known

remnants of Theodore's commentary, cf. W.F. Macomber, *Muséon* 81 (1968) 441; I am not sure to what extent he has actually collated the materials.
At first blush I dismissed the idea of a connection with the "Questions of Theodore" as preserved in Coptic, Arabic, Ethiopic; cf. A. van Lantschoot, *Studi e Testi* 192 (1957). In spite of my reluctance to get involved in such a delicate issue, John Strugnell prodded me into some further looking around. In *Muséon* 71 (1958) 279 f. van Lantschoot announced materials beyond the original 23 questions. The Syriac extracts in our MS are materially different, but bear a certain typological affinity. It stands to reason that scribes easily added the *mefašqānā* epithet to any 'Theodore' they encountered, and such attributions have to be checked by specialists. Cf. note on MS Syr 93.

[3] For almost a century it is known (cf. Gottheil, *Hebraica* 5 (1889) 215 f) that the texts published originally as *Opuscula Nestoriana* appear in various forms and extracts. Note Wright, *Catalogue ... Cambridge*, (1901) 546. Gottheil had access to the MS which I have now catalogued as MS UTS Syr 19 in the appendix to this catalogue.

[4] I am aware that this could be another author, Joseph Huzaya, and I have not checked that problem. If we judge by its contents, the extracts seem to fit Hazzaya's writings — but I do not feel I want to get involved in this kind of analysis. Cf. the paper by A. Guillaumont, *L'Orient Syrien* 3 (1958) 3 f.

Syr 73 [formerly: SMH 63, access 4001; Cl 108]

TWENTY FIVE HOMILIES BY JACOB OF SERUG AND ONE BY APHREM; ca 17 cent; Serto; partly mixed vocal; 246 fol; 22 × 16 cm; paper; incomplete.

Details: Index in later hand fol 1; Aphrem's homily on faith 209*b*–213*b;* for identification of selection: the MS contains homilies on the paralytic, love of poor, centurion, poor widow, prodigal son, etc.[1]

[1] The MS has recently been mentioned in Vööbus, *Handschriftliche Überlieferung der Memre-Dichtung des Ja'qob von Serug, CSCO* 344/5 *Subsidia* 39 (Louvain, 1973) 61; cf. MS Syr 100.

Syr 74 [formerly: SMH 64, access 4002; Cl 109; PM p. 54]

LITURGICAL PSALTER, SYRIAC AND GARSHUNI;[1] 1986 Sel; Serto; occasional Western vocal, but spirant throughout; mostly 3 col; 223 fol; 27 × 21 cm; paper; complete (leaves misplaced).

Details: The third column contains exegetical excerpts from many writers as well as occasional readings from the Syro-Hexapla and "massoretic" notes; the main exegete quoted is Bar Ṣalibi, often from his 'spiritual' commentary; Canticles start 206*a* followed by Nicene Creed, Gloria, Beatitudes, etc. (similar hand, no notes); further canticles — Hanna, Habakkuk, Isaiah, etc. 218*b*.

[1] According to the terminology suggested for MS Syr 5 the term 'liturgical psalter' has been used. The colophon uses ܟܬܒܐ ܕܡܙܡܘܪ̈ܐ ܕܚܘܫܒܢܐ ܗܢܐ. This is one of the rather rare cases where the colophon spells out ܗܘܫ ܕܩܫ̈ܝ ܘܡܫܝ̈ܚ.

Syr 75 [formerly: SMH 65, access 4003; Cl 110]

THIRTY TWO CHAPTERS FROM THE INTRODUCTION TO PSALMS BY BAR KEPHA[1] AND THE COMMENTARY TO PSALMS BY DANIEL OF TELLA; 2066 Sel; Serto; occasional mixed vocal; 242 fol; 22 × 16 cm; paper; complete.

Details: Commentary by Daniel of Tella 38*b*.

[1] The first part of this codex was edited by Diettrich, *BZAW* 5 (1901), who did not identify the author. On the basis of other MSS (cf. also MS Syr 130 fol 95*a*) Moses Bar Kepha has been identified. Cf. also Vosté, *RB* 38 (1929) 214; but there remain some open questions.

Syr 76 [formerly: SMH 66, access 4004; Cl 111]

A SELECTION OF HUMOROUS AND MOVING STORIES; 19 cent; Nestorian; vocal; 87 fol; 22 × 16 cm; paper; complete.

Details: Selections from the 'Laughable Stories' by Bar Hebraeus 2*b*; 'moving stories' collected by Deacon Jeremiah 38*b*; story of the building of Mossul 80*b*; last page contains notes in Arabic and Syriac concerning the conquests of Bagdad and Jerusalem.

Syr 77   [formerly: SMH 67, access 4005; Cl 112]

SOLOMON OF BASRA: BOOK OF THE BEE — THE HISTORY OF SALVATION; Elul 1893 C.E.; Nestorian; vocal; 105 fol; 23 × 16 cm; paper; complete; cf. MS Syr 66.

Syr 78   [formerly: SMH 68, access 4006; Cl 113]

JACOB OF BARTELLA[1] — KNOWN ALSO AS SEVERUS BAR SHAKKO: THE BOOK OF TREASURES — A THEOLOGICAL 'SUMMA'; 2200 Sel; Serto; occasional mixed vocal; 193 (+3) fol; 22 × 15 cm; paper; complete.

Details: Colophon (192*a*) followed by two epistles of the author and a prayer.

---

[1]   This is a good illustration of my decision not to remark, as a rule, on differences between this catalogue and earlier descriptions. It would appear that Harris thought that the name ܒܪܬܠܝ signifies: Bar Talia. That curious mishap was copied by Titterton and by Clemons. The facts are known from standard sources such as Assemani, *B. O.* II 237; Wright, *Catalogue ... Cambridge* I, 425. Cf. MS Syr 126, 127. If I remember correctly, the name of that village was pronounced in modern times *Bartli*.
To confuse matters a bit more, there was a prolific scribe of the same name (cf. Mingana p. 362), who is possibly identical with the scribe of our MS Syr 111, 124, 127. That scribe adopted the habit of using the same kind of self-descriptive formula which was often used by his famous namesake. Again, just an illustration what kind of questions one could go into in a catalogue.

Syr 79 [formerly: SMH 69, access 4007; Cl 114]

A COLLECTION OF THEOLOGICAL TREATISES, EPISTLES AND
DISCOURSES;[1] 18 cent; Nestorian; partly vocal; 179 fol; 22 ×
14 cm; paper; incomplete.

Details: Selections from the third part of the Paradise by
Palladius 1*b;* epistles and *sententiae,* partly by Nilus 103*b;*
discourses by Abraham Naphteraya 116*d;*[2] epistles 132*b;*
admonitions and sayings by Abba Macarius 138*a;* questions
addressed to the Elders 152*a;* epistles 178*a.*

[1] There exists no study on the problem of "collections"; headings or
colophons can be an indication, but are certainly not decisive. This
volume is described (1*b*) as follows: ܪܠܝ ܕܬܪܝܢܐܕ ܐܠܗܐ ܡܢ ܕܝܬܝܪܐܕ ܐܠܗܐ
ܐܘܣܪ ܐܬܘܠܡܘܕ ܠܠܕܬ ܡܢ ܗܘܬܐܕ ܡܪܝܡ ܡܪܐܝܬ ܐܠܗܐܪܠ ܩܘܣܝ, ܐܠܗܐܩܠ ܐܬܘܠܡ ܬܠܗܐ
ܐܕܪ. This looks like an "index-heading," not like a literary unit.
[2] Cf. Mingana 1176 for various forms of this name.

Syr 80 [formerly: SMH 70, access 4008; Cl 115]

THE STORY OF AHIQAR;[1] Elul 1898 C.E.; Nestorian; 20 (+20)
fol; 23 × 18 cm; paper; complete.

[1] Harris noted that this is a copy of MS Urmia 270 (termed S_4 in
the edition) and that readings had been entered from MS Urmia 117
(=S_5). It is obvious that this copy served in connection with the 1913
edition. However, no sign can be found of collations from MS Urmia
115, 230 which should also have been available (cf. the Saru-Shedd
catalogue of 1898). Materials towards a further study of the
intriguing history of Syriac Ahiqar traditions have been outlined in
my text-exercise *The Wisdom of Ahiqar* (Jerusalem 1965). I have not
been able to find out what exactly is included in an edition of the
Arabic and Syriac texts published by G.B. Behnam, Bagdad 1976.
The Arabic publication by Anis Fariha (Beirut 1962) contains
nothing of textual interest.

Syr 81 [formerly: SMH 71, access 4009; Cl 116]

THE BOOK OF HIEROTHEOS;[1] 2106 Sel; Serto; occasional mixed vocal and partly spirant; 2 col; 119 fol; 22 × 16 cm; paper; complete.

Details: Creed; Lord's prayer (in "Turkish Garshuni"); conundrum (1*a*); admonition by Theodosius of Jerusalem, serving as Introduction 3*b;* Stephen Bar Ṣudailē's Hierotheos with scholia in the marginal column, mainly by Bar Hebraeus and Theodosius 8*a;* treatises on practice and faith of Armenians, some by Aphrem and Jacob of Serug 105*b.*

[1] Cf. the introduction to Marsh's edition (1927).

Syr 82 [formerly: SMH 73, access 4010; Cl 117]

HISTORY OF THE VIRGIN AND RELATED HOMILIES; 17–18 cent; Serto (different hands); occasional mixed vocal; 214 fol; 13 × 8 cm; paper; incomplete.

Details: End of Book six and addition 183*a;* homilies 189*a.*

Syr 83 [formerly: SMH 74, access 4011; Cl 118]

BAR HEBRAEUS: BOOK OF RAYS; Kanun II 2089 Sel; Serto; vocal and spirant; 179 fol; 23 × 16 cm; paper; complete.

Details: Colophon mentions collaboration of two scribes; binding made by using dozens of leaves of slightly older paper codices, partly of prayers and homilies; leaves of binding loose and partly legible.

Syr 84 [formerly: SMH 75, access 4012; Cl 119]

BOOK OF SERVICES AND PRAYERS; ca 13 cent; cursive Estrangelo; 2 col; 72 fol; 36 × 26 cm; vellum; incomplete.

Details: Some later marginal additions, some Arabic; edges damaged and text partly faded; colored geometrical ornamentation fol 58*a*, naming deacon Jacob (?) as scribe.

Syr 85 [formerly: SMH 76, access 4013; Cl 120]

A COLLECTION OF PRAYERS AND HOMILIES, MAINLY IN CONNECTION WITH FUNERAL SERVICES; ca 12 cent;[1] 150 fol; 30 × 21 cm; vellum; incomplete.

Details: This is not exclusively an order for funerals like MS Syr 49, but also here part of the biblical texts are Syro-Hexaplaric admixtures;[2] main part — fol 10*b*-146 — includes Funeral Services (10*b*), homilies by Aphrem and Jacob of Serug (44*b*), further services (59*a*), discourses by the above and Isaac of Antioch (114*a*); fragments from different Service Books, partly illegible and bound lengthwise fol 1–3, 147–150.

[1] Some damaged and missing leaves were supplemented in a partly vocalized Serto; a note fol 9*a* states that the parts of the MS were put together Ḥziran 1808 Sel.
[2] Cf. the paper mentioned Introduction, above n. 1. Thus Num XX fol 27*a*, Jer XVIII fol 30*b*.

Syr 86 [formerly: SMH 77, access 4014]

A VOLUME OF "APOCRYPHAL" AND THEOLOGICAL TREATISES IN GARSHUNI; Tishrin II 1890 C.E. (see fol 136*b*); Serto; 194 fol; 25 × 18 cm; paper; complete.

Details: Apocalypse of Peter 2*a*;[1] discourse by Aphrem 137*a*; parts from Bar Hebraeus: Book of lightnings — the concise compendium of dogmatics 142*b*;[2] a short history of the councils (*mağāmi'*) of the church and the schism 164*b*; tracts on faith, fasts and commercial activities 184*b*; calendar tables for fasts, starting 2193 Sel 191*b*.

[1] The title is in this case ܘܠܩܐ ܐܘܪܝܠܘܢ ܐܬܪܠܐ ܝܕܗܪ; for different forms cf. e.g., Cat. Berlin p. 736, Mingana p. 793.
[2] The heading which describes this as an abbreviated version of the *Candelabrum of Sanctuaries* is, of course, not quite correct.

Syr 87 [formerly: SMH 79, access 4015; Cl 121]

A VOLUME OF HYMNS AND PRAYERS; 1883 Sel (note fol 105*a*, 134*a*); Serto; partly mixed vocal (partly later hand); 231 fol; 21 × 15 cm; paper; incomplete.

Details: Daily services 1*a*;[1] magnifical hymns[2] 45*b*; vigils 59*b*; mystic hymns, eight orders of supplications and cathismatha 98*b*; hymns by Aphrem 156*b*; further prayers and hymns, partly by Aphrem 200*a*.

[1] The note fol 45*b* describes these as ܪܬܐܘܢܐ ܪܬܠܐܪܐ ܪܝܬ. I may have misread the second term, and I do not know what prayer it refers to.
[2] These are ܪܕܠܩܐ ܪܬܐܘܢ.

Syr 88 [formerly: SMH 80, access 4016; Cl 122]

FUNERAL SERVICES AND RELATED HYMNS; ca 17 cent; inelegant Serto; partly mixed vocal; 140 fol; 18 × 13 cm; paper; incomplete; Oriental wood and leather binding (with inscriptions).[1]

[1] For the use of non-Peshitta texts cf. MSS Syr 49, 85. Only this manuscript claims expressly that those are non-Peshitta texts (fol 51*a*): ܗ ܝܪ .... ܪܕܬܘܪܐܘ ܪܕܩܢܐܕܬܐ ܪܬܝܝܗ ܪܬܠܐ ܕܗ ܪܠܬܐ ܠܬܐ ܠܬܐ ܘܐܩ ܝܠܬܬܢܝ.

Syr 89 [formerly: SMH 81, access 4017]

A COLLECTION OF TWENTY ONE ECCLESIASTICAL TRACTS, DIS-
COURSES AND 'HOLY STORIES' IN GARSHUNI;[1] 17–18 cent; Serto;
147 fol; 18 × 13 cm; paper; complete.[2]

Details: Index 1*a*;[3] dialogue between Moses and God on Sinai
1*b*; Euphrosyne 8*a*; King Zeno 15*a*; the leper in the time of
Jesus 32*b*; the drachmas of Judas Iscariot 38*a*; the apple 40*b*;
Elisa on presents 45*a*; discourses by Evagrius (56*b*), Aphrem
(74*a*), Jacob of Serug (110*a*), Chrysostom (128*a*); the second
letter from Heaven 139*a*.

[1] A later hand has subtitled the volume on the last leaf: ܟܬܒܐ
ܕܬܫܥܝܬܐ ܕܩܕܝܫܐ ܡܪܢ ܒܝܠܦ. Cf. note on MS Syr 74.
[2] Although there is a colophon that mentions the place (near
Aleppo), I cannot find a notation of the year.
[3] This is one of the few volumes for which Harris prepared
indexing slips; cf. MS Syr 99.

Syr 90 [formerly: SMH 82, access 4018]

A COLLECTION OF FIVE ECCLESIASTICAL TRACTS AND STORIES
IN GARSHUNI; 18 cent; Serto; 82 fol;[1] 16 × 11 cm; paper;
complete.

Details: Story of Isaiah of Aleppo 1*a*; fifth chapter of the *kitāb
ar-ru'ūs*[2] 24*a*; first letter from Heaven 27*a*;[3] dialogue between
Moses and God on Sinai 40*a*; canons of Apostles and Fathers
53*a*; prayers 80*a*.

[1] Apart from the first five leaves, the folios have not been
renumbered. The last entry starts fol 80*a* (=82*a*).
[2] I would think this is a Garshuni version of the work attributed to
Isaac from the convent of Rabban Īšō'; Baumstark, *GSL* p. 224 is
probably superseded by Chabot, *Muséon* 59 (1946) 345 f.
[3] It should be remembered that Bittner, *Denkschriften d. kais.
Akademie der Wissenschaften Wien,* 51 (1906) 138 used the Garshuni
version from this manuscript.

Syr 91 [formerly: SMH 83, access 4019; Cl 123]

A VOLUME OF MONOPHYSITE POLEMICAL TREATISES AND EPIS-
TLES, MAINLY BAR ṢALIBI'S 'ANTI-HERETICAL' TRACTS; 1898
C.E.;[1] Serto; partly mixed vocal; 2 col; 420 fol; 30 × 20 cm;
paper; complete.

Details: Index to treatises of Bar Ṣalibi against Arabs, Jews,
Nestorians, etc. 4*b;* against Arabs 11*b;* against Jews 60*a;*
against Nestorians 76*b;* second disputation against Nestorians
94*a;* index to treatise against Greeks (Chalcedonians) 145*b;*
against Greeks I 155*b;* against Greeks II 209*a;* epistle by
'Orthodox' bishops 292*b;* further index 296*b;* against Armenians 297*a;* related tracts and epistles against Armenians, also
by John Bar Shushan and John Bar Andreas 318*b;* discourses
by the Fathers on sacrifices 386*a;* further epistles by Bar Ṣalibi
and Bar Shushan 390*a;* passage from Josephus on the second
destruction of Jerusalem 408a.

[1] There are colophons fol 93*b,* 155*b,* 333*a;* fol 1*a* in Garshuni.
Notes of scribes copied from a *Vorlage* fol 4*a,* 11*a.* It seems somewhat
astonishing that no such volume of Bar Ṣalibi's writings existed in the
major European libraries before the acquisitions by scholars like
Harris and Mingana. This volume served for deZwaan's publication
of the treatise against the Jews. The part against the Armenians,
including the polemic against Kewark, are more or less paralleled by
codices such as Mingana 215, 347. Cf. *Woodbrooke Studies* 4 (1931).

Syr 92 [formerly: SMH 84, access 4020; Cl 124]

EXTRACTS FROM THE *GANNATH BUSSAME,* CONCERNING MAR
ABBA;[1] 19 cent; non-professional Nestorian; partly vocal; 85
fol; 22 × 17 cm; paper; complete.

[1] From the correspondence left in the volume it transpires that this
copy was prepared for a specific purpose at the request of Harris
under the supervision of W.A. Shedd. Harris suspected some

74

references in connection with the Diatesseron literature and he had the commentary checked for that purpose. Harris had looked for a certain Mar Abba, a disciple of Aphrem. Instead he got references to a later churchman. Shedd in his letters to Harris, written in 1899, realized what happened and Harris explained the idea in a letter to Titterton in 1925. Cf. also the similar type of volumes, MS Syr 97, 101.

I might add that in the early fifties I had noted down for myself a query, whether the manuscript mentioned by Harris, *Horae Semiticae* 5, XVIII (cf. also 10, XII) as belonging to him is what was then Rylands 41. But I cannot check into this now. It is possible that the manuscript of the *Gannath Bussame* used by Shedd was Urmi 180 — which might be the one now kept in Princeton. All such details remain to be checked. For the Urmi manuscript see W.F. Macomber, *ZDMG Suppl.* I:2 (1969) 478, n. 35. For the textual tradition of the Gannath Bussame cf now Reinink, Muséon 90 (1977) 103.

Syr 93 [formerly: SMH 85, access 4021; Cl 125]

A VOLUME OF "APOCRYPHAL" AND ECCLESIASTICAL WRITINGS;[1] 8–9 cent; Estrangelo, 92 fol; 24 × 16 cm; vellum; incomplete and partly damaged.

Details: Questions of Addai and answers of Jacob 1a;[2] questions of Thomas[3] and answers of Jacob 33b; questions of John the stylite from al-Yathrib and answers of Jacob 37a; replies by Fathers 44b; Gospels of the Twelve Apostles[4] 47a; further extracts from the "Teaching of Addai" and the anti-Nestorian discourse of Severus 58a; extracts from "Apostolic canons" and canons of various synods (Nicaea, Ancyra, Antioch, etc.) 60a;[5] questions addressed to Tymothy of Alexandria and further extracts 89b; significance of names of heavenly powers 92a.

[1] The manuscript was described and partly published by Harris in his *The Gospel of the Twelve Apostles* (1900).
[2] For the details cf. Baumstark, *GSL*, 83. Harris marked in the

75

manuscript itself that the beginning corresponds to the text in Lagarde, *Reliquiae iuris eccl.* (1856) 124.

[3] Because of the problem referred to above (MS Syr 72) I should add that these are the usual kind of "halachic" questions addressed by a certain ܡܫܐܠܢܐ ܕܡܫܐܠ — no more.

[4] This part is entitled ܐ[ܘ]ܪܚܬܐ ܕܝܢ, ܕܘܡܝܐܠܘ ܘܥܠܝ̈ܬ ܥܠ[ܗ]ܬܒܝ̈ܢ ܐܝܢܝܠܘ ܒܗܘܢ.

[5] The subscription fol 89*b* sums this part up: ܥܠܝ̈ܬ ܕܚܝܢܐ ܕܫܠܝ ܕܕܐܪ̈ܟܐ ܘܕܥ̈ܐܪ ܘܕܫܘܐܠܐܬܗ ܠܗܘܢ.

Syr 94   [formerly: SMH 86, access 4022]

A VOLUME OF "APOCRYPHAL" WRITINGS AND "HOLY STORIES" IN GARSHUNI; 2157 Sel (cf. fol 51*a*, 75*b*); Serto (different hands, partly inelegant); 77 fol; 22 × 15 cm; paper; incomplete.

Details:[1] Prayer (in Syriac) and writing exercise 1*a*; Apocalypse of Paul 2*b*; story of the king's son 38*b*; Mary the Repentant 43*b*; changing of kingdoms by Mutadawi of Rome 45*a*; fate of the faithful after the dispersion 52*a*; story of the Virgin 75*b*.

[1] Also for this volume index slips by Harris are extant.

Syr 95   [formerly: SMH 87, access 4023; Cl 126]

NESTORIUS: PRAGMATEIA OF HERACLIDE;[1] Kanun II 1899 C.E.; Nestorian; vocal; 140 fol (Syriac pagination); 36 × 21 cm; paper; complete.

[1] The copy was prepared for Shedd and he added notes and corrections. For the fate of copies from an Urmi *Vorlage* cf. the introduction to Luise Abramowski, *Untersuchungen zum Liber Heraclidi des Nestorius*, CSCO 292, subs. 22 (1963).

76

Syr 96   [formerly: SMH 88, access 4024; Cl 127]

ANAPHORAE, PARTLY IN GARSHUNI; 1846 C.E.[1] Serto; partly mixed vocal and spirant; 141 (+4) fol; 23 × 15 cm; paper; complete.

Details: Instructions for celebration of the Eucharist 2*b;* Anaphorae of St. James, John the Evangelist, St. Peter, St. Matthew 47*b;* further liturgy for the Eucharist 96*a;* Anaphorae of John of Nisibis 123*b;* Vigil of the virgin 135*b.*

[1] This is one of the early 19 cent copies, prepared in Tur Abdin; cf. detailed colophon 135*a.*

Syr 97   [formerly: SMH 89, access 4025; Cl 128]

EXTRACTS FROM THE *GANNATH BUSSAME* CONCERNING EXEGESIS ATTRIBUTED TO APHREM;[1] 19 cent; non-professional Nestorian; partly vocal; 28 fol; 23 × 18 cm; paper; complete.

[1] The manuscript is similar in every respect to MSS Syr 92, 101.

Syr 98   [formerly: SMH 90, access 4026; Cl 129]

BAR HEBRAEUS: BOOK OF POEMS; 2209 Sel; Serto; partly mixed vocal and spirant; 213 fol; 19 × 12 cm; paper; complete; detailed colophon.

Details: Fol 142*b* starting additional poems and hymns by Aphrem, Jacob and Simon the Catholicus.[1]

[1] Initial heading has the customary "in the meter of Mar Jacob" (6*a*). Such superscriptions easily turn into "by", and detailed checks are needed. The hymns 147*b*, 171*a* are expressly said to be "by."

Syr 99 [formerly: SMH 91, access 4027: Cl 130]

A VOLUME OF "APOCRYPHAL" AND ECCLESIASTICAL TREATISES AND EXCERPTS;[1] Nisan 2210 Sel; Serto; partly mixed vocal; 201 fol (399 in Arabic pagination); 26 × 19 cm; Western paper with lines; complete.

Details: Didascalia Apostolorum 1*b;* first epistle of Clement to the Corinthians 76*b;*[2] epistle of Jacob of Jerusalem to Quadratus 92*b;* letters of Herod and Pilate 93*b;* "memorials" of Jesus 96*b;*[3] doctrine of Peter 103*b;* epistle by Dionysius of Athens 107*a;* extracts from Epiphanius, Severus, Philoxenus, Xystus, Chrysostom, etc, 111*b.*[4]

[1] The colophon sums it up as ܪܬܐܠܝܗܢ ܪܘܚ̈ܝܕ ܪܠܢܡܪܝܗܢ ܪܬܠܐ
.... ܡܣܠ ܝܗܢ ܪܚ̈ܝܒ. For the literary problem of such collections cf. note 1, MS Syr 79.

[2] This was dealt with in an excursus which Titterton added to his draft.

[3] It would seem that the texts published by Ignatius Ephraem II Raḥmani, *Studia Syriaca* (1904) ought to be compared.

[4] These are dozens of very short extracts culled from the writings of all the main authorities of the Monophysite Orthodox Church. Some are polemical (against Chalcedonians and Nestorians — 122*b*), some philosophical (132*a*). There are headings which would facilitate proper identification.

Syr 100 [formerly: SMH 92, access 4028; Cl 131]

FORTY TWO HOMILIES BY JACOB OF SERUG; 2211 Sel (see fol 49*b,* 126*b*); Serto; partly mixed vocal; 2 col; 192 (+4) fol; 41 × 29 cm; paper; complete.

Details: Index 3*b.*[1]

[1] Cf. the recent study of A. Vööbus, *Handschriftliche Überlieferung der Memre Dichtung des Jacob von Serug, CSCO* 344/5 (1973) 112; cf. MS Syr 73.

Syr 101   [formerly: SMH 95, access 4030; Cl 133]

EXTRACTS FROM THE *GANNATH BUSSAME* CONCERNING EX-
EGESIS ATTRIBUTED TO THEODORE OF MOPSUESTIA;[1] 19 cent;
non-professional Nestorian; partly vocal; 110 fol; 23 × 17 cm; paper;
complete.

[1]   Cf. notes on MS Syr 92, 97. Note also MS Syr 72.

Syr 102   [formerly: SMH 96, access 4031; Cl 134]

BOOK OF SERVICES AND PRAYERS FOR SUNDAYS AND FESTIVALS;
12–13 cent; cursive Estrangelo; 2 col; 307 fol; 35 × 25 cm;
vellum; incomplete; partly damaged.

Syr 103   [formerly: SMH 97; access 4032; Cl 135]

BOOK OF SERVICES AND PRAYERS FOR SUNDAYS, FESTIVALS AND
SPECIAL DAYS;[1] 12–13 cent; cursive Estrangelo; 2 col; 388 fol;
45 × 31 cm; vellum; incomplete; partly damaged.

Details: Some hymns ascribed to Aphrem and Jacob of Serug;
some marginal notes by later hands; note fol 203*b* mentions
scribe Stephen.

[1]   From the description of MSS such as 102, 103 it should be
assumed that these are the kind of volumes often referred to as
"choral services."

Syr 104   [formerly: SMH 98; access 4033]

DAMAGED FRAGMENTS FROM TREATISE ON CANONS FOR MONKS,
IN GARSHUNI; 16–17 cent; Serto; 2 col; 5 fol; 24 × 16 cm;
paper.

Syr 105 [formerly: SMH 99, access 4034; Cl 136]

DAMAGED FRAGMENTS FROM COLLECTIONS OF CANONS; 16–17 cent; Serto; partly vocal and spirant; 7 fol; 24 × 16 cm; paper.

Syr 106 [formerly: SMH 100, access 4035; Cl 137]

DAMAGED FRAGMENTS FROM ECCLESIASTICAL AND EXEGETICAL EXTRACTS; 16–17 cent; Serto; partly mixed vocal and spirant; 6 fol; 24 × 16 cm; paper.

Details: Discourse by Gregory Nazianzen on baptism; epistle of Ignatius; commentary on I Thessal.

Syr 107 [formerly: SMH 101, access 4036; Cl 138]

A COLLECTION OF "HOLY STORIES"; 19 cent; partly mixed vocal; 20 fol; 26 × 20 cm; European paper with lines; partly damaged.

Details: Story of Euthalius 1*a;* story of Ignatius of Antioch 6*b;* eight youths of Ephesus 11*b.*[1]

[1] This is the text sometimes termed "The Seven Sleepers." The superscription in some sources (cf. Wright, Cat ... Cambridge p. 586) talks expressly of eight youths and our text counts all eight by name in the superscription.

Syr 108 [formerly: SMH 102, access 4037; Cl 139]

A BOX CONTAINING DAMAGED FRAGMENTS, MOSTLY FROM BINDINGS;[1] 16–18 cent; inelegant Serto; partly Garshuni or Arabic.

Details: Different books of prayer; psalter; "Holy Stories," Garshuni prayer; Garshuni paraphrase of Genesis; marriage ritual; homily of Jacob of Serug; Persian and Arabic fragments.

[1] The contents are arranged at present in 19 files which in no way agree with what was there in Titterton's draft. By their very nature these fragments can only be identified with much effort. The details indicate very roughly what can be found in the files. The contents are similar to that of MS Syr 109.

Syr 109 [formerly: SMH 103, access 4038; Cl 140]

A BOX CONTAINING DAMAGED FRAGMENTS, MOSTLY FROM BINDINGS; different centuries, some 14 cent; mostly inelegant Serto.

Details: Fragments from books of prayers, hymns; part from a letter of Heaven in Garshuni; part of an early Syriac-Latin printed text.

Syr 110 [formerly: SMH 104, access 4039; Cl 141]

A BOX CONTAINING DAMAGED FRAGMENTS FROM THREE BOOKS OF SERVICES AND PRAYERS;[1] 12–14 cent; cursive Estrangelo; altogether over 100 fol; 48 × 36 cm; vellum.

[1] As opposed to MS Syr 108 and MS 109, this box contains not small units but singed remnants of super-folio codices plus a few loose leaves, partly slightly earlier. The fragments are now repacked in four large envelopes. My notes from 1960 indicate that at that time they were wrapped in Boston newspapers from 1923, i.e., the time when Titterton was studying.

Syr 111 [formerly: SMH 105, access 4040; Cl 142]

A COLLECTION OF DISCOURSES AND EPISTLES ON WISDOM, LARGELY BY BAR HEBRAEUS; 2200 Sel (see 107*b*); Serto; partly mixed vocal; 2 col; 119 (+6) fol; 23 × 17 cm; paper; complete.

81

Details: Bar Hebraeus: The talk of wisdom — the short compendium on logic and metaphysics with a Garshuni version in parallel column[1] 4*b;* questions and replies — mostly by Bar Hebraeus, partly by John Bar Ma'dani 72*b;* poem on divine wisdom, with commentary 111*a.*[2]

[1]   The edition by H.F. Janssens of the ܪܘܫܐ ܣܘܡ (Liège 1937) does not contain the Garshuni version.
[2]   I have checked Titterton's suggestion referring to *Cat ... Oxford* p. 371, and the *incipits* fit. Hence the "Syrian philosopher" of our MS may well be Bar Hebraeus.

Syr 112 [formerly: SMH 106, access 4041; Cl 143]

A COLLECTION OF TREATISES BY MOSES BAR KEPHA (AND ONE BY JOHN OF DARA);[1] Ab 1894 C.E.; Serto; partly mixed vocal; 2 col; 126 (+10) fol; 33 × 23 cm; paper; complete; some colored geometrical ornamentations; detailed colophon in Garshuni and notes 45*a,* 68*a.*

Details: Index 5*b;* soul 6*b;* resurrection 45*b;*[2] angels 68*b;* paradise 95*b;*[3] the chapter by John of Dara on demons (90*b*) seems to have been joined sometimes with Bar Kepha's treatises on the creation of angels and angelic order.[4]

[1]   The volume as a whole is termed ܟܬܒܐ ܕܡܚܝܢܘܬ ܒܪ ܐܠܗܐ.
[2]   There has been a problem for some time whether the treatise on resurrection was written by Bar Kepha or by John of Dara. Cf. recently in W. Strothmann, *Moses Bar Kepha: Myronweihe, Göttinger Orientforschungen* I:7(1973) 25.
[3]   This will illustrate again the problem that within the framework of a catalogue one cannot check all the sources. It seems astonishing that Bar Kepha's treatise on the paradise should not have survived elsewhere in a European library. But this seems to emerge from Baumstark, *GSL,* p. 281. Mingana MS 65 C is probably an excerpt; but the uncatalogued MS Syr Yale 10 seems to give us the text of the work which was known from Masius' translation only. Cf. Migne, *Patrologia Graeca,* CXI, 481–608.
Vööbus *HTR* 68(1975) 378 f. has now described the differences

between this MS (which contains only two books of the "paradise" and MS Syr 118. According to him (p. 381) MS Syr 47 is still the most ancient copy of Bar Kepha's "resurrection" now in our possession.
Of course, also other writings of Bar Kepha did not survive in Europe, according to Baumstark — but that was before Mingana 9 (Mingana 480 is a short excerpt). Similarly, John of Dara's Treatise would not seem to exist in Syriac; Titterton referred to Cambridge Add 3285; but that is in Garshuni. In short, one has to check very carefully whether claims for uniqueness can be sustained. In light of recent discoveries in Church libraries (Vööbus, Macomber, etc.), such uniqueness seems rather unlikely and just before this volume went to the printers my suspicion was borne out; cf. Vööbus, *JAOS* 96 (1976) 577.
[4]   Apart from MS Syr 118 cf. also the above Cambridge MS 3285, fol 169a.

Syr 113   [formerly: SMH 107, access 4042; Cl 144]

DISCOURSES AND EPISTLES BY PSEUDO-DIONYSIUS (DIONYSIUS THE AREOPAGITE); Nisan 2205 Sel;[1] Serto; partly mixed vocal; 2 col; 183 (+10) fol; 31 × 23 cm; paper; complete.

Details: Introductions by translator etc. and prefaces 5b; divine names 25b; heavenly hierarchy 102b; mystical theology 132a; ecclesiastical hierarchy 137a;[2] ten epistles 169b.

[1]   As in the case of MS Syr 66 and 67, one may remark on the fate of this and the preceding codex. Both were written in 1894 by a certain Deacon Matthew in Mosul and have stayed together ever since. It is possible that MS Syr 114 was penned by the same scribe, ten years previously. Again, were one to follow up all the information for stemmatic purposes, one would note the fact that this MS is said to have been copied from a 1078 Sel *Vorlage* — which gets us to the neighborhood of the *Vorlage* of one of the British Museum MSS. In spite of the fascination that such exercises hold, they must be left for those scholars who will actually study the MSS in depth.
[2]   For the general side, outside the Syriac, cf. the recent study in *The Greek Orthodox Theological Review* 19 (1974) 173 f. Cf. also G. Wiessner, *NAWG* 1971.

Syr 114   [formerly: SMH 108, access 4043; Cl 145]

BAR HEBRAEUS: THE ASCENT OF MIND — A BOOK ON AS-
TRONOMY; 1884 C.E.; Serto; partly mixed vocal; 120 (+4) fol;
23 × 16 cm; paper; complete.

Details: Index (uncounted leaves);[1] ascent 1*b;* credo by Bar
Hebraeus in Garshuni 110*a;* detailed colophon 107*a.*

[1] The Arabic and Syriac pagination does not include the initial
index.

Syr 115   [formerly: SMH 109, access 4044; Cl 146]

A VOLUME OF 'SPIRITUAL' TREATISES AND EPISTLES BY JOHN OF
DALYATHA ('JOHN SABA');[1] Teshrin II 1889 C.E.; Serto; partly
mixed vocal; 124 (+10) fol;[2] 23 × 17 cm; paper; complete;
initial rubrication damaged.

Details: Exhortatory discourses, mostly on monastic life, the
senses and "hidden knowledge" 7*b;*[3] fifty-one epistles 56*b;*
discourses on knowledge 97*a;* Sunday observance 108*a;*
alphabeth 112*a;* exhortation 124*a;* end of main collection
126*a;* between the author and his brother 127*a;* exhortations
by Jacob of Serug 129*b.*

[1] The colophon talks of ܟܬܒܐ ܗܢܐ ܕܝܠܝ ܕܝܘܚܢܢ, but that is hardly a
title. Also the subscription fol 126*a* is only descriptive. Cf. MS Syr 42.
Cf. in general the recent study by B. Collers, "The Mysticism of John
Saba," *OCP* 39 (1973) 83f. Note also P. Sherwood, *L'Orient Syrien 1*
(1956) 305f.
[2] MS starts fol 7.
[3] The subscription fol 56*b* may refer to the last item or to the
whole: ܫܠܡܘ ܕܪܫܐ ܡܐܠ̈ܐ ܗܘ̈ܝ ܕܗܘܐ ܫܘܡܗ. For the subject of "Syrische
Verordnungen für die Novizen" in MS Syr 42 fol 41*b,* MS Syr 115
fol 66*b,* cf. Vööbus, *Oriens Christianus* 54 (1970) 109.

Syr 116 [formerly: SMH 110, access 4045; Cl 147]

THE COMMENTARY OF APHREM ON THE OLD TESTAMENT; Adar 1899 C.E.; Serto; partly mixed vocal; 2 col; 159 (+10) fol; 40 × 28 cm; paper; complete.

Details: The commentary on Genesis is followed by a collection of exegetical notes from both Aphrem and Jacob of Edessa on Genesis 26a–29a.[1]

[1] The problem of the "combined" commentary by Aphrem and Jacob still needs study. The same unit reappears in MS Syr 123, written by the same scribe.

Syr 117 [formerly: SMH 111, access 4046; Cl 148]

"THE CAUSE OF ALL CAUSES," ATTRIBUTED (BY TRADITION) TO JACOB OF EDESSA; Teshrin II 2205 Sel; Serto; partly mixed vocal; 205 (+9) fol; 23 × 16 cm; paper; complete.

Details: Each of the seven discourses preceded by its index.

Syr 118 [formerly: SMH 112, access 4047; Cl 149]

A COLLECTION OF TREATISES BY MOSES BAR KEPHA (AND ONE BY JOHN OF DARA);[1] 2064 Sel; Serto; partly mixed vocal; 253 fol; 33 × 23 cm; paper; complete.

Details: Soul 2b; resurrection 82a; angels 125b; angelic order 148b; demons — by John of Dara 165a; paradise 174b.

[1] Cf. MS Syr 112. I have not checked the statement of Titterton that, generally speaking, the present MS is superior, even though both seem to depend on a common ancestor. Note the recent evaluation of Vööbus mentioned above, MS Syr 112.

Syr 119 [formerly: SMH 113, access 4048; Cl 150]

TREASURY OF MYSTERIES — THE SCHOLIA OF BAR HEBRAEUS ON THE BIBLE;[1] Iyar 2174 Sel;[2] Serto; partly mixed vocal; 348 fol; 21 × 15 cm; paper; composite-complete.

[1] Note the discussion by W.C. Graham, *AJSL* 41 (1925) 102f.
[2] There exists a problem as regards the evaluation of slightly different dates written in the margin. The MS is made up from different parts, largely ca 17 cent. It would seem that it received its final form at the above date, or some eight years later.

Syr 120 [formerly: SMH 116, access 4051]

BAR ṢALIBI: COMMENTARY ON THE GOSPELS, IN GARSHUNI; Teshrin I 2118 Sel; Serto; 363 (+35) fol;[1] 33 × 21 cm; paper; complete.

[1] According to the Syriac pagination in the MS, fol 5*b* equals p. 1.

Syr 121 [formerly: SMH 118, access 4053; Cl 154; PM p. 7]

THE OLD TESTAMENT IN THE PESHITTA RECENSION: A BETH MAWTᵉBHE VOLUME; ca 14 cent; Nestorian Serto;[1] partly mixed vocal; 184 fol; 26 × 18 cm; paper; incomplete; cf. MS Syr 137.

Details: Starting Jos 1:8 (fol 1–3 ca 16 cent); Jud 9*a*, Sam 22*b*, Reg 68*b*, Prov 118*a*, Sir 136*b*, Eccl 165*a*, Ruth 172*a*, Song 175*a*, Job 178*a*; sections marked in margin; partly damaged and leaves missing.

[1] This is one of the instances where script labels are misleading and where one wishes for a detailed colophon. According to the literary character, one would expect Nestorian letters. Yet the script is a very particular type of semi-angular Serto which is only faintly similar to the usual Nestorian. Cf. MS Syr 135; bMS Syr 152.

By the way, ancient *Beth Mawt'bhe* volumes are much rarer than one suspects; this volume is possibly the fifth oldest in existence. I do not know on what authority the authors of the Leiden PM spell *Beth Mawtabhe*. The American missionaries who worked in Persia a century ago got the local pronunciation as *Bit Mitwee;* cf. the orthography used by Perkins in the description pasted into MS AOS Rn B 47 B (Yale-Beinecke).

Syr 122 [formerly: SMH 119, access 4054; Cl 155]

A COLLECTION OF THE WRITINGS OF JOHN OF DARA: PARTLY FROM HIS COMMENTARIES ON PSEUDO-DIONYSIUS;[1] Kanun II 2210 Sel; Serto; partly mixed vocal; 2 col; 185 (+4) fol; 35 × 23 cm; paper; complete.

Details: Heavenly hierarchy 2*b;* ecclesiastical hierarchy 18*b;* four discourses on priesthood 40*a;* four discourses on resurrection 66*b;* sacrifice and Eucharist 159*b;*[2] explanation of creed 176*b;* designation of priest and deacon 180*a.*

[1] A preliminary comparison suggests that this MS is particularly similar to Vat 100 and Mingana 56.
[2] Cf. now A. Vööbus, "Important Manuscript Discoveries — Iwannis of Dara," *JAOS* 96 (1976) 576 f, who refers to this MS and to the edition *CSCO, Scr. Syri* 132 (1970).

Syr 123 [formerly: SMH 120, access 4055; Cl 156]

JACOB OF EDESSA: COMMENTARY ON PARTS OF THE OLD TESTAMENT;[1] Shbat 1903 C.E.; Serto; partly mixed vocal; 115 (+4) fol; 24 × 17 cm; paper; complete.

Details: This volume includes scholia on the Pentateuch, Job, Joshua and Judges; the 'shorter commentary' by Aphrem and Jacob on Genesis (including some additional quotes from Fathers) starts 64*a.*

[1] Cf. MS Syr 116. The exact of nature of the 'scholia' must be restudied. The superscription to this MS states that this comes from the "shorter" version — ܪ̈ܘܚܩܠܕܐ ܐܝܟ. The books are those enumerated Baumstark, *GSL* p. 250.

Syr 124 [formerly: SMH 121, access 4056; Cl 157]

SIXTY DISCOURSES BY ISAAC OF ANTIOCH;[1] Adar 2209 Sel; Serto; partly mixed vocal; 2 col; 187 (+3) fol; 28 × 20 cm; paper; complete.[2]

[1] Titterton had already pointed out the similarity with MS Berlin 162. Differences of internal ordering as compared with ed. Bedjan (1903) need further study. Also Assfalg, *Syrische Handschriften*, No. 17–18 should now be compared.
[2] For the scribe, Jacob of Bartella (who loved to append detailed colophons), cf. note on MS Syr 78.

Syr 125 [formerly: SMH 122, access 4057; Cl 158]

FIVE DISCOURSES ON RHETORIC BY ANTONIUS RHETOR OF TAGHRITH;[1] Teshrin II 2207 Sel; Serto; partly mixed vocal; 103 (+10) fol; 24 × 16 cm; paper; complete.[2]

[1] ܐܢܛܘܢܝܣ ܪܗܛܘܪܐ ܕܬܓܪܝܬ.
[2] Lacunae in text are due to damaged *Vorlage:* the text was published in reduced photographic reproduction by Sprengling, *AJSL* 32 (1916) 145f.

Syr 126 [formerly: SMH 124, access 4059; Cl 160]

JACOB OF BARTELLA (KNOWN ALSO AS SEVERUS BAR SHAKKO): THE BOOK OF DIALOGUES — A TREATISE ON RHETORIC, GRAMMAR AND ELOQUENCE — PRECEDED BY SOME EPISTLES ATTRIBUTED TO BAR ṢALIBI;[1] Kanun I 2207 Sel; Serto; partly mixed vocal; 135 fol; 23 × 16 cm; paper; complete.

Details: Five epistles attributed to Bar Ṣalibi 2*b*;[2] three discourses of the Book of Dialogues 5*b*.

88

[1] This volume was mentioned by Sprengling, *AJSL* 32 (1916) 303. A letter by Furlani is folded into the volume.
[2] I have not checked the authenticity. The name of the author has been entered secondarily. Another epistle is included fol 135*a*.

Syr 127 [formerly: SMH 126, access 4061; Cl 162]

JACOB OF BARTELLA — KNOWN ALSO AS SEVERUS BAR SHAKKO: THE BOOK OF TREASURES; Kanun I 2214 Sel; Serto; occasional mixed vocal and spirant; 211 fol; 21 × 15 cm; paper; complete.

Details: Cf. MS Syr 78; fol 207*a* start two epistles by the author.

Syr 128 [formerly: SMH 127, access 4062; Cl 163]

FRAGMENTS FROM EXODUS IX–XIV IN THE PESHITTA RECENSION; 16–17 cent; semi-professional Serto; 5 fol; 18 × 13 cm; paper.

Details: Ex 9:25–14:8.

Syr 129 [formerly: SMH 128, access 4063; Cl 164]

PARTS OF THE HISTORY OF THE VIRGIN;[1] ca 17 cent; Serto; partly mixed vocal; 2 col; 83 fol; 21 × 15 cm; paper; incomplete and partly in disorder.[2]

[1] Only a fullscale study of the various constituent parts of "History of the Virgin" collections will clarify the manifold issues involved. While sometimes the term "Revelation of Theophilus" seems to be used for a whole collection, it is doubtful whether that term should be adopted. What is now fol 20*a* bears the subscription ܠܝ ܡܘܬܐ ܗܝܠ ܟܘܠܠܗܘܐܬ(!)ܐ ܡܫܝܚ ܐܘܢܐ; cf. Mingana 5:39.
[2] Psalms XXV–XXVIII appear fol 25–26 in direct continuation between Books 4 and 5.

Syr 130 [formerly: SMH 129, access 4064; Cl 165]

BAR SALIBI: COMMENTARY ON THE OLD TESTAMENT — SPIRITU-
AL AND MATERIAL;[1] Shbaṭ 2199 Sel (see 315*b*); Serto; partly
mixed vocal; 2 or 3 col; 318 fol; 39 × 28 cm; paper; complete;
colored geometrical ornamentation after detailed colophon.

Details: Introduction to Psalms by Moses Bar Kepha 95*a*–103*a*;
commentary of Aphrem on Maleachi and Joel 317*a*.

[1] The known codices have recently been enumerated by Vööbus,
ZAW 84 (1972) 246f; our MS is mentioned p. 249. I am afraid that
the project mentioned in this connection in my paper *Bulletin John
Rylands Library* 37 (1955) 444 is in abeyance. The Syrohexapla
quotes, however, can be handled now with much greater confidence.

Syr 131 [formerly: SMH 130, access 4065; Cl 166]

ISHO'DAD OF MERV: COMMENTARY ON THE NEW TESTAMENT;
Tamuz 1904 C.E.; Nestorian; partly vocal; 240 fol; 30 × 20
cm; paper; complete.[1]

[1] The list prepared for the Semitic Museum upon transferral of the
collection by Harris states that this is one of the MSS kept by Harris
after the transaction. It was shipped to America about a decade later
(April 1915). The reason was, of course, that it was used. Its use in
the framework of volumes published by Mrs. Gibson as *Horae
Semiticae* 5–7 is set out in the introduction to those volumes. Notes on
various verses were written on the margin (by Harris?) and later
erased. The Urmi MS from which this one was copied is lost. Cf. MS
UTS Syr 17.

Syr 132 [formerly: SMH 131, access 4066; Cl 167]

A VOLUME OF TRACTS ON PHYSICS AND MEDICINE, IN THE MAIN
— JOB OF EDESSA: BOOK OF TREASURES;[1] 1904 C.E. (see 188*b*);
semi-professional Serto; partly mixed vocal; 194 fol; 28 × 20
cm; paper; init. incomplete.

Details: Questions and answers on physics and medicine by Alexander of Aphrodisias 2*b*;[2] questions and answers on medicine by Galen 36*a;* Job of Edessa on canine hydrophobia 48*b;* Job of Edessa: Book of Treasures — a compendium in six parts on sciences, theology and philosophy 52*b*;[3] Ḥunain the physician: four elements 188*b;* extracts on dreams, the heart, the brain 193*b.*

[1] Especially Mingana 559 should be compared.
[2] I am not sure whether anybody has ever counted the full 220 items this treatise is said to include. This treatise is preceded by the end of some tract dealing with knowledge(?).
[3] Mingana published the text of his MS in *Woodbrooke Scientific Publications* I (1935). The contents are paraphrased in the subscription to our MS as: ܪܘܡܢܐ ܟܠܘܗܝܐ ܘܐܦܐ ܘܥܝܠܐ ܪܒܐ ܠܝܢ ܐܒܐ ܩܢܐ ܡܠ ܚܠܐ ܬܚܬܢ ܩܠܐ ܠܝܢ ܡܘܠܐܝ ܠܝ ܐܝܟ ܩܠܐ.

Syr 133   [formerly: SMH 132, access 4067; Cl 168]

ANAPHORAE — PARTLY IN GARSHUNI OR WITH GARSHUNI TRANSLATION; Iyar 2060 Sel; Serto; partly mixed vocal and spirant; 2 col; 70 fol; 31 × 22 cm; paper; complete.

Details: Ornamental index (partly damaged), introductory lessons and prayers 1*a;* twelve anaphorae (St. James,[1] St. Peter, Apostles, etc.) 12*b;* epilogue and homily 65*a;* detailed colophon 67*a.*

[1] Cf. on this subject G. Khouri-Sarkis, *L'Orient Syrien* 4 (1959).

Syr 134   [formerly: SMH 133, access 4068; Cl 169; PM p. 54]

PSALTER AND CANTICLES, WITH INTRODUCTIONS, EXEGETICAL NOTES AND TRACTS — PARTLY WITH "TURKISH GARSHUNI"

RENDERING; 19 cent; Serto; mixed vocal and spirant; 2 col;[1] 179 fol; 47 × 31 cm; paper; incomplete.

Details: Introductory extracts (from Hippolyte, Epiphanius, Isaac of Nineveh, etc. 1*b;* Psalms and notes 3*b;*[2] Canticles 159*b;* extracts from Bar Hebraeus (on Lord's Prayer), Bar Salibi (on Nicene Creed), Athanasius, etc. 165*b;* sections for services indicated.

[1] I do not recall Syriac psalters with a Turkish version. It is, perhaps, no coincidence that for most of the volume the Turkish column has been left blank.

[2] The particular arrangement of notes in this volume is said to be according to the ordering (ܐܝܟ ܛܟܣܐ ܕܬܪܬ ܡܪܝ) of Athanasius. I do not know whether this relates to the considerable number of variants "according to the Greek" noted in the margins. A study of Syrohexaplaric readings from Bar Hebraeus and Bar Salibi would have to peruse this MS carefully.

Syr 135 [formerly: SMH 134, access 4069; Cl 170]

LITURGICAL PSALTER; 16–17 cent; Nestorian;[1] vocal; 134 fol;[2] 22 × 16 cm; paper; incomplete.

Details: Start with Ps 38:13; Canticles 93*a;* hymns for sundays, festivals, etc. by Doctors of the Church[3] 98*b,* lent services 113*a,* extracts from canons 127*a.*

[1] Also for this script the label "Nestorian" is not sufficient; cf. MS Syr 121. There is a certain resemblance to the script of MS Syr 152, but it is different. Specialists in liturgy will note the division into ܗܘܠܠܐ which seems the usual Nestorian one (end of MS missing). There is no sign of καθίσματα. I would assume that a Melkite connection is excluded, both because of the division and the vocalization. But I have some problems in comparing the hand of MS Syr 173.

[2] Syriac pagination in MS starts with p. 62. This indicates loss of about three initial quires. Last leaf of MS added by different hand.

[3] ܕܡܠܦܢܐ ܕܥܕܬܐ ܕܩܕܝܫܐ .... ܘܡܪܝܐ ܕܐܒܗܬܐ ܕܩܕܝܫܐ ܘܡܘܪܒ.

92

Syr 136   [formerly: 501;[1] Cl 174; PM p. 54]

PSALTER; 1697 C.E.;[2] Serto; vocal; 108 fol (Syriac pagination in MS); 21 × 14 cm; paper; complete.[3]

[1]   This is the first MS beyond the old sequence of the Semitic Museum list, as mirrored in the notes by Titterton. MS Syr 136 and all subsequent numbers were transferred to Houghton at various times — some of them had simply remained in the Semitic Museum for no apparent reason. When I tried to get some order into the collection and to have it kept in one place, back in 1960, I myself started off by numbering 501, simply to start a series of numbers not used elsewhere in the collection. Scholars who consulted the MSS afterwards have used those numbers. Since certain SM MSS had been missing, I kept 511, 513 open in order to relate to an existing sequence. In the event SM 2192 did turn up after years — but at that point there was no reason to reemploy the vacant number. For these reasons some of the following items will show former SMH numbers, others will not. In 1970 the present system of numbering was finalized, as indicated in the introduction.

[2]   The date looks reasonable. But the ductus of the colophon raises some doubts. The scribe comes from the Tarablus area and describes himself as one of the priests serving under the metropolitan Buṭrus al-Bustani.

[3]   A note on the fly leaf states that the codex belonged to a priest in the Maronite church in Damascus and was bought by B.S. Wolcott in Beirut in 1851. It is one of the few MSS which came into the Harvard College Library directly — as part of the A.S. Wolcott bequest, 1923.

Syr 137   [formerly: 502; SM access 1076; Titt p. 14; Cl 18; Go *Textus* 2:52]

THE OLD TESTAMENT IN THE PESHITTA RECENSION: A BETH MAWTᴱBHE VOLUME; 10–11 cent;[1] Estrangelo; occasional Nestorian vocal; 172 fol; 24 × 16 cm; vellum; incomplete.[2]

Details: Reg, Prov, Sir, Eccl, Song preserved more or less fully; sections occasionally indicated in margin; starts Jos 18:20; Jud

6*b;* Sam 24*a,* Reg 67*a,* Prov 112*b,* Sir 129*b,* Eccl 155*b,* Ruth 161*a,* Song 163*b,* Job 165*b.*

[1] With the possible exception of Paris Syr 372, this is as early a copy of a *Beth Mawťbhe* volume as we possess. However, MS AOS Rn B47 B is possibly a bit earlier. I should like to point out that that MS (Yale-Beinecke) has a considerable amount of original Nestorian vocalization.

[2] These are loose, brittle and partly singed leaves in a box — many sequences missing. This is the copy used by G.F. Moore for his commentary on Judges; cf. his Introduction, p. XLVII and see MS Syr 138. Bloch, *AJSL* 37 (1920) 143 is only a second hand mention. The SM access entry for May 22, 1893, when SM bought the codex, informs us: "Moore bot this of J.P. Peters and he of H.B. Meyer."

Syr 138   [formerly: 503; SM access 1077;[1] Ti p. 15; Cl 19]

THE NEW TESTAMENT IN THE PESHITTA RECENSION; 11–12 cent; cursive Estrangelo; occasional Nestorian vocal; 175 fol; 22 × 15 cm; vellum; incomplete.[2]

Details: The volume is made up from two MSS, roughly coeval; the second hand (a proper Estrangelo) starts fol 144; some sections indicated in margin and some marginal additions; Matthew 1*b,* Mark 11*a,* Luke 29*b,* John 63*a,* Acts 91*a,* James 118*b,* Hebrews 171*a,* fragments from Eusebius tract on the "Seventy" 173*a.*

[1] On the binding cloth from within, there are faint traces of what looks like Sem Mus 75. I tend to take this as one of the "forgotten" numbers. The MS was bought by the SM in 1893 from G.F. Moore; cf. note on MS Syr 137. It is damaged, partly singed, and what remains of it is placed in a box.

[2] This MS was mentioned shortly after its purchase by SM in *The Independent* NY, 7 June 1894: 734 e. Hence it came to the knowledge of C.R. Gregory, *Textkritik des neuen Testaments* (1902) 1297.

94

Syr 139   [formerly: 504; SM access 2198; Ti p. 16; Cl 20]

GOSPEL LECTIONARY IN THE HARKLEAN RECENSION; ca 12 cent; large Estrangelo; 2 col; 158 fol; 44 × 28 cm; vellum; incomplete and severely damaged;[1] some colored illuminations.

Details: Portions indicated in text and on margin.

[1] A crater-shaped large hole has burned through half the MS. An accompanying note mentions that the MS was damaged during a pogrom in Armenia in 1895. It seems that after it was rescued it found its way to America. In 1900 the SM bought it from James Barton, together with MS Syr 140.

Syr 140   [formerly: 505; SM access 2199; Ti p. 19; Cl 21]

BOOK OF SERVICES AND PRAYERS;[1] ca 12 cent; large cursive Estrangelo; 2 col; 222 fol; 47 × 34 cm; vellum; incomplete; damaged; loose in a box.

[1] This is the kind of codex that would be described as: Choral Services for the year; cf. Introduction.

Syr 141   [formerly: 506; SM 2[1]; Ti p. 6; Cl 22]

GOSPEL LECTIONARY IN THE PESHITTA RECENSION FOR SUNDAYS AND FESTIVALS;[2] Ḥziran 1519 Sel; Estrangelo; partly Nestorian vocal; 2 col; 167 fol;[3] 35 × 25 cm; paper; complete (slightly damaged).

[1] According to the list of accessions this is the first Syriac MS that came to the Semitic Museum. A label on its binding reads 22A. This

95

is not a SM notation and probably predates its acquisition by
Harvard. It was bought in 1890 from W.A. Shedd.
[2] Titterton's remark that this MS is very similar to BM CCXLVIII
ought to be verified.
[3] Two fragmentary leaves of prayers and stories bring the total to
169 fol.

Syr 142   [formerly: 507, SM access 43;[1] Ti p. 10; Cl 17]

'GAZZA' — THE CHALDEAN FESTAL ANTIPHONARY;[2] Adar 1978
Sel; Nestorian; vocal; 588 fol; 31 × 20 cm; paper; complete;
Oriental wood and leather binding.

[1]   The analysis of the accession numbers shows that also this MS was
acquired in 1890. The accession numbers cover, of course, items
other than MSS. This codex was presented by Mrs. E.A. Burleigh.
Apparently it came via the usual mission channels from Urmia.
It is of some interest that in the early days of the Semitic Museum
this was regarded as the most valuable Syriac codex. Cf. the remark
made by Lyon in his description of the SM holdings, *JAOS* 15 (1893)
ci: "... Further, Syriac, Arabic and Hebrew manuscripts; of the first,
the finest is the *Gezza*, containing lives of Syrian saints; it is of a
thousand pages and written in 1666 ..."
[2]   Different terms are being used and specialists may be aware of
differences in rites. This codex is termed in the colophon as follows:
ܪܠܘܬܐ ܕܐܬܪܐ ܕܓܐܘܬܐ ܕܠܝܢܐ ܕܒܝܬ ܡܠܐܢ ܕܩܐܘܪܒܬܘܟܐ ܐܠܝ
....ܪܝܬܐܘܬܬܐ. Also in this case the rite is that of the "upper
monastery" of Mar Gabriel and Mar Abraham in Mosul. The
heading uses also the usual ܪܐܨܬܘ ܡܫܐܠ. It should be noted that the
name of the monastery where this codex was written has been erased
(fol 586*b)*. Cf. for the rite the details of MS Syr Camb Add 1980. For
some unusual rite cf the recent remarks of W.F. Macomber in *A
Tribute to Arthur Vööbus* (Chicago 1977) 332.

Syr 143   [formerly: 508; SM access 2190; Cl 47][1]

A VOLUME OF THEOLOGICAL TRACTS, EXHORTATIONS AND PARAPHRASES FROM BIBLICAL TEXTS;[2] 2200 Sel (fol 96*a*); Nestorian; vocal; 103 (+6) fol;[3] 27 × 20 cm; paper; complete.[4]

Details: Exhortations and "ascetic" tracts 3*a;* metered instruction for novices[5] 47*a;* ceremonies and explanation of mysteries[6] 52*a;* rhymed paraphrases from Prov, Sir, Eccl 59*a;* polemical exhortation by John Bar Zo'bi 87*a;* Holy Stories 93*b.*

[1] MSS Syr 143–149 are all modern and unbound paper codices, kept in one box. None of these was seen by Titterton, but they were numbered by me in 1960 and consequently seen by Macomber. I should point out that among the accession numbers of these MSS, No. 2192 is missing. For some reason this MS stayed behind in SM and was transferred to Houghton only in July 1970 when I prepared the pre-final draft of this catalogue.

[2] Since the description fol 96*a* as ܟܬܒܐ ܕܫܥܝܘܬܐ ܕܩܕܝܫܐ occurs also 87*a*, this is hardly the title. Colophon in this and following MSS partly in modern Syriac.

[3] Most of these MSS have European or Syriac pagination and even mention the Urmia College.

[4] Considerable lacunae because of omission in *Vorlage.*

[5] ܬܘܒ ܐܡܪܝܢܢ ܥܠ ܕܝܠܗ ܗܘ ܕܝܢ ܕܟܠ ܝܘܡ.

[6] ܥܠ ܬܫܡܫܬܐ ܘܡܥܡܘܕܝܬܐ ܘܩܘܪܒܐ ܐܠܗܝܐ.

Syr 144   [formerly: 509; SM access 2188; Cl 45]

FRAGMENT OF BOOK OF SERVICES IN MODERN SYRIAC;[1] 19 cent; Nestorian; partly vocal; 134 fol (Syriac pagination in MS); 22 × 18 cm; paper; incomplete.

[1] The language seems to be literary standardized Urmi as used by the Protestant mission in its publications; but I have not checked for telltale "isoglosses." Macomber, *OCP* (1970) 120f. seems to suggest that this was a more or less academic exercise of rendering the *Ḥudra,* in conformity with Protestant tendencies at the time. Cf. MS Syr 147.

Syr 145 [formerly: 510; SM access 2189; Cl 46]

METRIC LIFE STORY OF RABBAN HORMIZD, THE PERSIAN; Nisan 1889 C.E.; Nestorian; partly vocal; 99 fol; 27 × 20 cm; paper; complete; cf. MS Syr 67, UTS MS Syr 20.

Details: Also this MS has colophon in modern Syriac (and European pagination).

Syr 146 [formerly: 512; SM access 2191; Cl 48]

HISTORY OF ALEXANDER; Iyar 1889 C.E.;[1] Nestorian; partly vocal; 125 fol (European pagination); 27 × 20 cm; paper; complete.

[1] This is the date p. 249; the date p. 246 (1885) does not refer to this MS; colophon in modern Syriac.

Syr 147 [formerly: 514; SM access 2193; Cl 49]

GOSPEL LECTIONARY FOR SUNDAYS AND FESTIVALS, IN MODERN SYRIAC;[1] Kanun I 2199 Sel; Nestorian; vocal; 102 fol; 27 × 20 cm; paper; complete.

[1] Cf. note on MS Syr 144. From heading and colophon (partly modern Syriac) together we learn that this is termed ܟܬܒܐ ܕܩܘܪܝܢܐ ܕܝܠܗܘܢ ܥܕܢܐ ܕܩܝܡܬܐ ܕܡܪܢ ܘܕܥܐܕܐ ܘܕܟܠܗܘܢ ܝܘܡܬܐ ... ܠܡܫܡ ܒܠܫܢܐ ܕܗܘܐ ܘܝܕܝܥ ܘܩܪܝܐ ܐܝܟ ܕܡܫ ܠܟܠ ... The heading names the translator: ܗܘܫܥܐ ܕܝܫܘܥܐ ܝܘܣܦ ܐܘܪܡܝܐ. While I did not study MS Syr UTS 15 concurrently, I think this is the same version. My notes leave me in some confusion whether I intended to note down that UTS 15 was copied from an 18 cent MS in Modern Syriac (in which case there is no connection with the American Protestant mission). This should be gone into by those who are interested enough in these issues.

Syr 148   [formerly: 515; SM access 2194; Cl 50]

TABLES FOR CALCULATING THE TIMES OF NEW MOONS AND RELIGIOUS FESTIVALS; 19 cent; Nestorian; 16 fol; 33 × 25 cm; paper.

Details: The tables cover a period of roughly one thousand years — before and after the time of this MS.

Syr 149   [formerly: 516; SM access 2195; Cl 51]

'ISAGOGE' AND COMMENTARY TO LOGIC[1] BY JOSEPH II, PATRIARCH OF THE CHALDEANS; 1885 C.E.; Nestorian; vocal; 66 fol; 18 × 11 cm; paper; complete.

Details: Commentary 16*a*; Index 65*a*.

[1]   The heading terms this ܪܕܘ܂ܬܐ܂ܕ ܪܕܗܐܠ܂ܠܬܐܕ ܪܠܐܘ܂ܓ܂ ܪܬܕܐ while the colophon refers to the part termed ܂ܢܝܐܠ ܕ܂ܐܕܐܢ ܪܝܐܛܘ܂ܪܬ ܪܕܝܐܕ. The heading of the commentary unit mentions that the text was rendered from Arabic. Wright, *Cat. Cambr.* p. 857 is aware of the existence of this treatise from Joseph's autobiography, but for the text itself MS Mingana 433 is to be compared.

Syr 150   [formerly: 517; SM access 1186; Cl 28]

FUNERAL SERVICES ACCORDING TO THE NESTORIAN RITES;[1] Adar 2098 Sel (fol 122*a*); Nestorian; vocal; 127 fol; 23 × 16 cm; paper; complete; Oriental wood and leather binding.

Details: Selections from synodal canons in the end of the volume 118*a*.

[1]   The MS described by Hall, *Hebraica* 4 (1888) 82f. is MS Syr UTS 10, not ours. Details of MSS such as Berlin 54, Camb 1985 differ to some degree.

Syr 151 [formerly: 518; SM access 2184; Cl 41]

LOOSE FRAGMENTS, SOME FROM BINDINGS AND PARTLY DAMAGED;[1] about 25 leaves from 10–12 MSS, mostly 1–3 leaves per unit; a few old fragments.

Details[2]: One leaf vellum, largely faded, ca 8 cent Estrangelo, 24 × 17 cm, contains part from letters of Abgar and Jesus as well as a discourse "Love of Poverty" numbered 37;[3] 1 large leaf, vellum, Estrangelo 37 × 25 cm, 2 col, from ca 10 cent lectionary; 1 large damaged leaf, vellum, cursive Estrangelo, 37 × 26 cm, from ca 10 cent Book of Commemorations;[4] fragment of upper part of 3 col leaf ca 13 cent Estrangelo, containing part of discourse 71 (?) for Passion Monday;[5] 1 double leaf severely damaged from 13 cent cursive Estrangelo, Book of Services, 40 × 28 cm; 2 leaves, 2 col, ca 11 cent Serto, 28 × 20 cm, from treatise on ecclesiastical law on canons (with some Greek terms in contemporary hand[6] on the margin); 1 leaf, 13 cent cursive Estrangelo from exhortatory tract (damaged); some 17–19 cent paper fragments from prayer books, etc.[7]

[1] These are kept in a box, together with MS Syr 152.

[2] This is not to detail all the fragments, but merely the more important ones.

[3] The text goes on and says: (! ܪܚܡ ܙܝ ܐܠܗܐ ܡܣܟܝܢܘܬ ܡܢ ܕܐܝܬ ... ܪܒܝܬܐ. I have not checked for identification. This item clearly shows that this is the lot of Clemons' "unlocated manuscripts," p. 511. Cf. Hall, *AJSL* 1 (1884) 232f.

[4] One heading probably refers to Jacob of Serug: ܥܠܘܗܝ ܟܬܒܐ ܕܣܘܓ.

[5] If I remember rightly this is the only 3 col leaf in the collection, 38 cm broad. This is a pretty rare way of writing, altogether. The author of the discourse is Mar Iwannīs (of Dara?).

[6] The problem of checking dating procedures through Syriac-Greek paleographic correspondences has not yet even been formulated.

[7] It seems that all the fragments — both the ancient vellum and the recent paper ones — were purchased by W.H. Ward in the area of Midyet in Tur Abdin. In 1885 they were sent to Isaac Hall. The accompanying letter is of some interest as regards prices in those days. It stands to reason that the fragments came to SM from the estate of Hall.

Syr 152 [formerly: 519; SM access 2183; Cl 40]

ISAAC ESHBADHNAYA: POEM ON THE DIVINE GOVERNMENT;[1] ca
17 cent; Nestorian;[2] 214 fol; 20 × 15 cm; paper; incomplete
and partly damaged; loose in Oriental wood and cloth
binding.

[1] This is the poem as described Cat. Cambr. Add 1998 which is
apparently identical with Berlin 85. Wright has raised the problem of
two different authors of *'Onīthās*, both named Isaac (E)shbadhnaya,
whereas Baumstark, *GSL* p. 330 knows them to be one. The
Mingana MSS seem to have materials only by the one called Asco.
But I do not propose to enter that discussion. Our volume is titled:
ܢܠܐ ܪܬܡܐܘ ܕܝܫܬܒ ܕܗ ܪܐܩܝܬܬܡ ܠܢܗ ܪܐܡܘܢܐ. I am not sure
whether some of the leaves do not belong to a different text.
[2] For the problem of script cf. MS Syr 135.

Syr 153 [formerly: 520; SM access 2175; Cl 32][1]

MANUAL FOR ORDINATION OF CLERGY, CONSECRATION OF AL-
TARS, ETC. — A 'BISHOP'S VADEMECUM';[2] Ab 2121 Sel; Nestorian; vocal; 196 fol; 22 × 16 cm; paper; complete; partly
damaged; loose Oriental binding.

Details: Consecration of altars with and without oil 2*b;* chalice
42*a;* procedures and canons for ordination 43*a;* rules for
monastic clothing;[3] sanctity of ablution;[4] further canons for
ordinations by 'Abd-Īšō' of Gᵉzartā (126*b*) and by Elias
Abuḥalim 132*a;* prayers for bishops 138*b;* consecration of
missionaries[5] 148*b;* final prayer over altar entrance[6] (and
others) 179*a;* final *'onītha*[7] 187*b;* a slightly different hand —
possibly the first owner — copied some additional notes,
mainly on impediments to marriage.

[1] This is kept in one box together with MS Syr 154, 155.

[2] This is quite neatly expressed by the title ܩܘܠܢ ܟܬܒܐ ܟܕܠܐ ܕܐܠܝܫܕܐ.

[3] This seems to refer to the clothes worn by the monks — ܟܐܒܠܐ ܕܐܪܝܠܝܗ.

[4] I would prefer to render ܟܕ̈ܝܐ ܫܗܩܒ as "consecration of washing vessels," but it needs someone acquainted with the ritual to get the meaning. It may be some ritual of "holy ablution" of the feet since the text ends by saying ܘܢܩܝܡ ܡܠ ܒܩܬܒ ܕܠܐ ܗܒܝܪܘ.

[6] I assume that the expression ܟܕܠܗܘ ܕܝܢ ܠܝܠ ܫܕܝ ܟܠܩ refers to a dimissory prayer connected somehow to the portal of the apse; but the details of ritual are unclear to me. For the archetonic internal division of the Church cf. the material in F. Heiler (ed.) *Die Ostkirchen* (1971) 540. I take this text to be the same as MS Berlin 41:23; but Sachau's description does not help either. Nor does Assfalg p. 81.

Syr 154 [formerly: 521; SM access 2176; Cl 33]

THE NEW TESTAMENT IN THE PESHITTA RECENSION; ca 16 cent; cursive Nestorian Estrangelo;[1] vocal; 336 fol; 18 × 13 cm; paper; incomplete; partly damaged and pages missing; Oriental wood and cloth binding.

Details: Starting Matthew 7 (added by later hand), Mark 64a,[2] John 114a, Acts 144a, James 191a, Hebrews 324a; different hands starting fol 169, 182.

[1] This is, again, a hand that looks like cursive Estrangelo — only not leaning towards a Western Serto but rather towards an Eastern development.

[2] A great many pages are missing, and I have not taken the trouble to identify the part taken up by Luke.

Syr 155 [formerly: 522; SM access 1187; Cl 29]

A MANUAL ('SACERDOTAL') FOR PRIESTS,[1] INCLUDING CANONS;
Ḥziran 2097 Sel; Nestorian; vocal; 110 fol; 23 × 16 cm;
paper; complete; Oriental wood and leather binding.

[1] Assfalg, *Syrische Handschriften etc.* (1963) No. 35 has arranged
materials for comparison of units of this type of manuscript. Perhaps
the term "Euchologion" would be suitable.

Syr 156 [formerly: 523; SM access 3;[1] Ti p. 7; Cl 23]

A BOOK OF CHARMS;[2] 18–19 cent; Nestorian; occasional vocal;
46 fol; 11 × 8 cm; paper; complete; some crude
illuminations.[3]

[1] It is clear that this and many of the following items belong to the
initial acquisitions of SM. Most of these were acquired in 1890
through W.A. Shedd, when the first lot came from Urmia. All the
tiny codices and scrolls MS Syr 156–173 are now kept in one box.
[2] The term is ܪܬܢ̈ܠܕܐ ܪܬܐܠܕܢ ܪܠܛܐܠܛܢܐܪ. In other cases ܪܬܐܠ
ܪܝܠܠܬܐ is used; again, in others, ܪܬܐܠܕܢ ܪܐܚܐܒܐ. In MS Syr 163
the title has been translated into English and written into the
manuscript.
[3] All the charm items are 18–19 cent, usually partly written
diagonally across the page. Some have headings appropriate for the
occasion, such as: against terror, for the sick, etc. These scrolls,
especially MS Syr 159, were discussed soon after their arrival at SM
by W.H. Hazard, *JAOS* 15 (1893) 284f. Cf. note on MS Syr 166. It
should be noted that in many of these MSS the beginning of the
Gospel of John can be found. Also, divine epithets often appear in
fixed "Hebrew" formulations such as ܚܐܐܢܐ ܪܐܠܙܐ ܡܠܡܪܝܪ ܡܠܡܐ ܪܝܟܒ
ܐܐܪܐܝ ܪܝܚܐ. All such details need to be studied.

Syr 157 [formerly: 524; SM access 1189; Cl 31]

A VOLUME MADE UP OF FRAGMENTS; partly loose, from various
Nestorian paper MSS, some rather unprofessional; faded and

damaged; 18–19 cent; partly vocal; ca 260 fol; average 17 ×
11 cm; in part Oriental wood binding.

Details: Mostly prayers, funeral services, theological tracts,
blessing of bride and bridegroom, third letter from Heaven;
partly Modern Syriac.

Syr 158   [formerly: 525; SM access 6; Ti p. 9; Cl 26]

A NARROW LONG PAPER STRIP CONTAINING CHARMS; 18–19
cent; Nestorian; partly vocal; 127 × 7 cm; some crude
illuminations.

Syr 159   [formerly: 526; SM access 5; Ti p. 8; Cl 25]

A NARROW LONG PAPER STRIP CONTAINING CHARMS; 18–19
cent; Nestorian; partly vocal; 200 × 6 cm; some crude
illuminations.

Syr 160   [formerly: 527; SM access 2181; Cl 38]

A BOOK OF CHARMS; 18–19 cent; Nestorian; 49 fol; 12 × 8 cm;
paper; complete; some crude illuminations.

Syr 161   [formerly: 528; SM access 2180; Cl 37]

A BOOK OF MAGIC, DIAGNOSIS AND PROGNOSIS OF ILLNESSES,[1]
ATTRIBUTED TO THE PROPHET DANIEL AND TO EZRA THE
SCRIBE; 18–19 cent; Nestorian; partly vocal; 34 fol; 11 × 8 cm;
complete; Oriental wood and leather binding.

[1] From the study of such treatises it appears that the illness was
diagnosed by using the letters of the name of the patient as well as
some dates. Cf. MS Syr 166.

104

Syr 162   [formerly: 529; SM access 4; Ti p. 7; Cl 24]

A BOOK OF CHARMS: 18–19 cent; Nestorian; 50 fol; 8 × 5 cm; paper; complete; some crude illuminations.

Syr 163   [formerly: 530; SM access 2182; Cl 39]

A BOOK OF CHARMS;[1] 2120 Sel; Nestorian; partly vocal; 66 fol; 10 × 7 cm; paper; complete; some crude illuminations; Oriental wood and leather binding.

[1]   In this MS the title has been rendered into English and written into the MS itself: Book of the Protection from everything evil and hostile.

Syr 164   [formerly: 531; SM access 2185;[1] Cl 42]

THE STORY OF MAR 'AZĪZĀ;[2] ca 18 cent;[3] Nestorian; partly vocal; 44 fol; 15 × 11 cm; paper; complete, but slightly damaged.

[1]   In the MS itself the number was originally 2183, then corrected to 2175, then to 2185. The MS consists of loose leaves.
[2]   The title is not quite legible, but one can decipher .... ܡܚܘܝ ܟ̣ܠܝܐܪ ,ܕܘܗ .... ܝܬܟ̣ܠܒܘܡ.
[3]   In the colophon fol 40*a*, the year is left blank. It seems possible that this is a 'local' product connected with the village of Zereni (?), where the MS was written and which boasted a monastery dedicated to Mar 'Azīzā.

Syr 165   [formerly: 532; SM access 7; Ti p. 9; Cl 27]

A NARROW LONG PAPER STRIP CONTAINING CHARMS; 18–19 cent; Nestorian; vocal; 185 × 6 cm; some crude illuminations.

105

Syr 166 [formerly: 533; SM access 2186; Cl 43]

A VOLUME OF "HOLY STORIES";[1] Ḥziran 1885 C.E.; Nestorian; vocal; 31 fol (European pagination); 23 × 18 cm; paper; complete; some corrections in the margin.

Details: Dialogue between Moses and God on Sinai p. 1; third letter from Heaven p. 13; George the martyr p. 27; story of Arsenius, King of Egypt p. 49; canons for festivals and commemoration days; prescriptions for magical cures p. 55.[2]

[1] The colophon describes this volume as ܟܬܒܐ ܕܬܫܥܝܬܐ ܩܕܝܫܬܐ. Notes in some of the MSS in this lot show (cf. also MS Syr 167, 170) that they were bought from the estate of Hall by Moore (in 1900?); cf. Introduction. Previous numberings are crossed out; those may have referred to Hall's private collection. Thus, e.g., the present codex was No. 96. Hall published the Arsenius text in *Hebraica* 6 (1890) 81f. and the letter from Heaven *JAOS* 15 (1893) 121f. In his 1893 publication Hall does not mention the fact that he had previously published from the volume. Hence I was led to assume that these were publications from different MSS. I do not think this is the case. On the other hand, he published a different "recension" of the letter from MS Syr 169. Cf. note 2 on MS Syr 38 and MS Syr 51.

[2] Cf. *JAOS* 15: 137. Note MS Syr 161.

Syr 167 [formerly: 534; SM access 2187; Cl 44]

A COLLECTION OF SYNODAL CANONS AS ARRANGED BY MAR DENḤĀ;[1] Nisan 1886 C.E.; Nestorian; partly vocal; 132 fol (European pagination); 22 × 18 cm; paper; complete; some notes in the margin.

[1] The colophon describes this as ܣܘܢܗܕܣ ܕܩܢܘܢܐ ܕܣܘܢܕ ܕܐܒܗܬܐ.

Syr 168   [formerly: 535; SM access 2177; Cl 34]

HISTORY OF THE VIRGIN; Iyar 2090 Sel; Nestorian; partly vocal; 112 fol; 16 × 10 cm; complete; Oriental wood and leather binding; some crude illuminations.

Syr 169   [formerly: 536; SM access 2179; Cl 36]

A COLLECTION OF APOCRYPHAL STORIES; 18 cent; Nestorian; partly vocal; 97 fol; 16 × 10 cm; paper; complete, but damaged in beginning; Oriental wood and leather binding; some illuminations.

Details: Apocalypse of Paul 1*b;* third letter from Heaven[1] 84*b;* hymn before communion 93*b.*

[1] Hall noted in the volume that he had published this part of the MS *JAOS* 1891; cf. notes on MS Syr 38, 166.

Syr 170   [formerly: 537; SM access 2178; Cl 35]

A COLLECTION OF MORNING PRAYERS FOR FESTIVALS AND COMMEMORATIVE DAYS, AS ARRANGED BY THE CATHOLICOS ELIJA III (ABUḤALIM);[1] Kanun I 1859;[2] Nestorian; partly vocal; 79 fol; 14 × 10 cm; paper; complete.

[1] For the term cf. e.g., Cat. Cambridge p. 121 and see Baumstark, *GSL* 289. Since I am not sure about facts of liturgy, I should note that Macomber in his notes talks of prayers for the vigil service. But why would that be the meaning of ܪܬܐ ܪܚܠ؟

[2] Reading ܟܢܘܢ. For some time I was sure that the letter is so slanted that the date is ܟܢܘܢ, but there exist Nestorian hands with strongly slanted *nun.* The date must be C.E. Hall received the volume in 1892 from a certain Rabbi Baba. As an aside, the title is usually spelled "Rabi" — to prevent misunderstanding.

107

Syr 171 [formerly: 550;[1] SM access 8375; Cl 171]

FRAGMENT FROM A GOSPEL LECTIONARY IN THE PESHITTA RECENSION, CONTAINING PARTS OF LUKE X, XII; ca 14 cent; Melkite Serto;[2] 2 col; 1 fol; 27 × 21 cm; vellum.

[1] My notes from 1960 indicate that I wanted to start a new series of numbering for this lot which was not connected to the acquisitions from Hall, numbered at the time up to 537. I left numbers unassigned for possible surprises, and started again with 550.

[2] I do not know of a paleographically decisive characteristic of a Melkite hand. The decision is up to the expert in liturgy, also as regards MS Syr 173; contrast MS Syr 153. In any event, this is neither the usual cursive "liturgical" Estrangelo nor 14th cent Serto. To be sure, dating is in such a case even more hazardous than usual. With regard to Melkite characteristics note F. Ludger Bernhard, *Chronologie etc.* p. 85, 113. Baumstark's notes in *Katalog Hiersemann* 500 (1922) remain unsurpassed. But I am not sure that anyone ever defined a fragment as Melkite on the basis of script alone.

Syr 172 [formerly: 551; SM access 8376; Cl 172]

FRAGMENT OF A HYMN ON MARTYRS; palimpsest 14–15 cent; Serto; 1 fol; 17 × 12 cm; vellum.

Details: Incipits after rubrication;[1] lower writing shows 2 col cursive Estrangelo ca 12 cent.

[1] *Incipit I:*

ܒܫܘܢ ܐܝܗ ܘܗܡ ܐܠ ܕܠܝܕܚܪܝ
ܕܟ ܐܝܢܚܝܚܐܘܢ ܣܡܝܕܐ ܘܓܟ ܕܟܬܫܚܘܟ

Incipit II:

ܓܠܐ ܕܪܘܥܒܐ ܕܥܡܝܗܐ ܩܝܝܥ
ܒܣܩܡ ܐܝܚܙܪ ܐ

Syr 173 [formerly: 552; SM access 8377; Cl 173]

FRAGMENT OF LECTIONARY FROM 1 REG VIII AND DAN IX IN THE PESHITTA RECENSION; Melkite Serto;[1] 14–15 cent; 1 double fol; 16 × 12 cm; vellum.

[1] See note on MS Syr 171.

108

Syr 174 [formerly: SM access 1188[1]; Cl 30]

MARRIAGE RITUAL ACCORDING TO NESTORIAN RITE;[2] Teshrin I
2099 Sel; Nestorian; vocal; 98 fol; 16 × 11 cm; paper;
complete; Oriental wood and leather binding; some colored
illuminations.

Details: Betrothal 2*b*; bride chamber 13*a;* vessels 40*b;* crowning 55*a;* main text preceded by notes (in later hand) on
impediments, at what times wedding rites should not be
arranged.

[1] These and the following items were either out of the original
numbering sequence or missing in 1960; in any case they were not
numbered into the 500 series.
[2] The colophon uses the term ܟ̈ܠܘܠܐ ܕܡܫܝܚܐ ܫܠܝܛ. The
'crowning' takes, of course, place in connection with the marriage.
Cf. Assfalg, *Syrische Handschriften etc.* No. 36.

Syr 175 [formerly: Houghton access *42 M-1867F; Cl 16]

SELECTED PASSAGES FROM THE GOSPELS[1] WITH SOME EXEGETI-
CAL GLOSSES IN MODERN SYRIAC (ṬIYARE);[2] Adar 2154 Sel;
Nestorian; vocal; 30 fol; 28 × 20 cm; paper; complete; A B C
F M.

Details: The selections consists of Matthew 4:23–8:32; Mark
15:11–16:20, Luke 14:20–15:32; John 2:1–3:21. This does not
seem to reflect any lectionary custom.

[1] I have no idea why Clemons p. 517 corrected himself and stated
that these are selections from the New Testament. As far as I can see
these are Gospel selections.
[2] The title names the dialect expressly: ܦܘܫܩܐ ܕܣ̈ܝܩܐ ܕܟܝܢ ܐܘܢܓܠܝܘܢ ܒܠܫܢܐ ܣܘܪܝܐ ܚܕܬܐ. For students of the dialect it should
be noted that the scribe comes from the village of Ashīthā in lower
Tiyare.

109

Syr 176 [formerly: SMH 115, access 4050; Ti p. 242; Cl 152][1]

THE GOSPEL OF JOHN IN THE HARKLEAN RECENSION: 1023 Sel;[2] Serto; 87 fol; 11 × 8 cm; vellum; complete (some leaves missing or damaged).

Details: Harklean "Massora" (*shemāhe*) 83a–87a, with Western vocal and spirant; some Greek marginal notes;[3] late medieval metal binding with superscription;[4] later Syriac scribbling on fly-leaf.

[1] From the very analysis of the numbering something can be inferred about the fate of this MS. I had marked it as lost in 1960 as well as on recount in 1969. That fact does not emerge from Clemons' list, since he never saw the MSS, anyway. By a most amazing coincidence, the day I sat down to start the pre-final draft of this catalogue in the summer of 1970, someone unknown appeared in the office of the SM, put the volume on the desk of a secretary and quickly disappeared.

Bearing in mind the history of transferrals to Houghton, it stands to reason that the MS had been borrowed before the mid-fifties — probably much earlier. Someone may have discovered in his (or perhaps his father's) library this item, borrowed and long forgotten, and decided to clean the slate. In any case, at that point (1970) I suggested to Dr. G. Ernest Wright, then curator of the SM, to transfer this volume — as well as what is now MS Syr 177, 178 — to Houghton. Because of its special character I then assigned to SM access 8255–8278 their place as final item in the collection. But other MSS may yet reappear.

[2] This is the one case in the entire Harvard collection where the date is of utmost interest for the paleography of Syriac as a whole. This MS is reputedly the oldest codex in the world written in Serto, a major point indeed. This is the information we get from the only textbook in the field, W.H.P. Hatch, *An Album of Dated Syriac Manuscripts* (Boston, 1946) plate XCV, who reckons the date as 1043 Sel. Since this MS had disappeared (I do not wish to suggest this was more than a coincidence) we would have had to abide by his judgment.

Titterton was content to report on the colophon (fol 87a) which

110

seemed to read ܪ‌‍ܝܘܢ܄ ܕ‍ܠ‍ܕܐ ܘ‍ܝܣܪܐ ܟ‍ܐ‍ܠܪ that ܪ‍ܝܘܢ܄ had been
added and that ܘ‍ܝܣܪܐ was written in place of a number erased.
Apparently, the orthography did not bother him. Hatch reasons that
the number was ܘ‍ܕܝܪܐ or ܘ‍ܝܣ‍ܝܪܐ, and by trying to identify the
patriarch (the name Athanasius is given), he opts for Sel 1043. The
trouble is that the beginning letter of that number (which was erased
and written over) was definitely ܕ and not ܪ. The space would allow
for, say ܘ‍ܝܪܕ as well as for ܪܪ‍ܡ ܕܠܕ. We are thus forced back to
dating by paleography what is allegedly the oldest dated Serto
manuscript. As far as our meager knowledge goes, the writing looks
like ca 1000 C.E. rather than ca 700.

I would suggest that the original date was intended as A. Sel, even if
not spelled out. That would have been almost self-understood. It was
the forger who thought it necessary to be explicit and hence added
ܪ‍ܝܘܢܬ܄. A date of ca 1000 C.E. might, of course, be construed by
assuming original ܘ‍ܕܠܕ or ܘ‍ܝܪܕ. Since I believe the date to have
been A. Sel, I opt for an original ܪܪ‍ܡ ܕܠܕ i.e., A. Sel 1303. This is
not the only possibility, but typologically acceptable.

There is an additional consideration. Had the original been, say,
ܘ‍ܕܠܕ the gain in turning that into ܘ‍ܝܣܪ (!) would hardly have been
worth the effort. To be sure, we cannot judge the motive, and the
forger was pretty much inexperienced to botch the job up the way he
did. So much for the state of the art of dating early Serto
manuscripts.

[3] I have tried to get advice on Greek paleography, but to no avail. I
understand that the kind of uncial hand used will not enable us to
date — assuming the Greek to be of the same time as the Syriac. Cf.
MS Syr 151.

[4] This MS is unique as regards its binding — another possible
reason for its long disappearance. The metal covers show some crude
pictures of Virgin, child, etc. on one side and a crucified Christ on
the other, superscribed INBI (!). There is a superscription in
"pierced" letters which looks half Syriac, half Arabic. These details
seem to point to a craftsman who had no knowledge of the
languages; but the study of the technique must be left to experts. I
have heard the tentative opinion that the binding is, in any event, of
no consequence to the dating of the MS.

As for letters pierced into metal, I recollect having seen some Syriac
metal tablets in the Madrid National (?) library, but I have not
followed this up.

111

Syr 177 [formerly: SM access 841]

A COMPOSITE VOLUME, BINDING TOGETHER VARIOUS UNITS, CONTAINING PRAYERS, HYMNS AND THEOLOGICAL TRACTS, SOME IN GARSHUNI; 18–19 cent; Nestorian; partly vocal; 141 fol; 9 × 6 cm; paper; incomplete; loose leaves, many missing; loose Oriental wood and leather binding.

Details: Many pages from collection of hymns arranged by Elia of Soba (beginnings of lines rubricated); main part of prayers starting 18*b*.[1]

[1] This part is entitled ܠܒܗܐ ܕܚܘܡܬܐ ܫܚܝܡܐ i.e., an *officium feriale.*

Syr 178 [formerly: SM access 2192]

DISCOURSES BY APHREM, FOR RECITAL ON THE "ROGATIONS OF THE NINEVITES";[1] Ṭabaḥ[2] 2198[3] Sel; Nestorian; vocal; 95 (+5) fol; 22 × 18 cm; paper; complete.[4]

[1] The title is given as ܟܬܒܐ ܕܡܐܡܪ̈ܐ ܕܒܥܘܬܐ ܕܡܬܩܒܠܝܢ ܡܢ ܡܐܡܪ̈ܘܗܝ ܕܛܘܒܢܐ ܡܪܝ ܐܦܪܝܡ ܕܡܬܟܫܦܝܢ ܘܡܬܠܚܡܝܢ ܠܡܪܝ ܪܒܝ ܝܩܝܪܐ ܒܨܝܪܐ ܕܝܬܩܪܘܢ ܒܡܠܝܢ ܬܠܬܐ ܝܘܡܬܐ ܕܒܥܘܬܐ ܕܢܝܢܘܝܐ. This volume thus specifically refers to the arrangement by Yaqira (cf. Baumstark, *GSL* p. 289). My old notes compared uncatalogued Rylands Syr 26, but this needs verification. I assume that to the lot of MSS one must add the MS mentioned by Macomber, *ZDMG* Suppl I (1969) 480.

[2] This is the only month named in modern Syriac, in the whole collection. Altogether, the use of non-classical names for the months is rare in MSS. There must have been a reason for not using "Ab."

[3] The scribe tried to correct the date, but the correction is not clear (2199?).

[4] From a slip of paper written in 1897 we learn that this kind of recently copied MS was then purchased for five dollars. Cf. note on MS Syr 143.

Syr 179   [formerly: SM access 8255–8278]

TWENTY FOUR SMALL UNNUMBERED[1] BOUND VOLUMES OF EX-
TRACTS FROM SYRIAC WRITERS, KEPT IN A BOX.

Details: All volumes are written in 19 cent European hands
and contain notes, word lists, extracts, etc.[2]

---

[1]   A few are consecutively numbered.

[2]   Mainly material which Harris had noted from his own work, some
volumes written by Robert Payne Smith, probably acquired by Harris.
Some material may be of interest for studying the compilation of the
Thesaurus. From some notes it appears that after Harris had sold his
collection he decided to give these volumes as a present. By 1931
Lyon noted that no individual numbers had been assigned. This is
still the case.

APPENDIX I

SYRIAC MANUSCRIPTS
IN THE ANDOVER-HARVARD LIBRARY

The reasons for including in this volume certain manuscripts apart from those kept in the Houghton library of Harvard College have been mentioned in the general introduction. It was almost a matter of chance which manuscript came at a certain time to one library or the other.[1] This appendix will deal with the volumes now kept at the Harvard Divinity School in the Andover-Harvard Theological Library.

In 1960–61 I had numbered the manuscripts which I could find in the Andover-Harvard (= AH) library. Those numbers are reflected in Clemons 175–178. In 1969–70 I managed to rediscover some further items and in 1977 yet another. Hence seven MSS can now be located at AH.

In the spring of 1977 new numbers were assigned to those MSS within the overall system of AH.[2] Hence what was MS Syr AH 1 is now AH MS 325, etc. I have retained various earlier shelfmarks in order to facilitate identification.

Also the arrangement of this collection, as it stands now, is my responsibility. I think that I have been able to account for all the MSS which were known, at one time or another, to be kept in that collection. Hence, this volume reflects all the holdings of Harvard.[3]

As explained above, I had no business writing the catalogue of the main collection, and I ended up describing other collections, for completeness' sake. Consequently, the descriptions in the appendices have been kept to the barest minimum of details.

---

[1] All MSS but No. 326 and 331 came from Hall's collection roughly at the same time when other items from his collection were purchased for the main collection. I do not wish to get involved in an

114

inquiry into the whereabouts of Hall's MSS; these appendices should help to clarify some of the questions raised in the list of "unlocated manuscripts" (Clemons p. 510f.).

[2] I am glad to say that I have had the cooperation of the previous as well as the present librarian at Andover-Harvard. The numbers were, of course, assigned by the librarian.

[3] To be exact, one additional item got into a third Harvard collection: Fogg 1939.188 (Clemons 407). This is a 19 cent letter, double fol, 21 × 13 cm, written in modern Syriac to Rev and Mrs. Stocking. This is a personal letter written to the missionaries by a local woman, Rachel from Ada.

AH MS 325 [formerly: AH Syr 1; And access 51950; Cl 175][1]

THE NEW TESTAMENT IN THE PESHITTA RECENSION; 1510 Sel in Alkosh;[2] Estrangelo; partly Nestorian vocal;[3] 269 fol;[4] 26 × 19 cm; vellum; complete; loose Oriental wood and leather binding.

Details: Matthew 2*b*; Mark 37*a*; Luke 60*a*; John 99*a*; Acts 130*b*; James 174*a*; Hebrews 255*a*; some leaves missing in sequence, later hands added prayers, ownership notices and scribblings on leaves in beginning and end, originally left empty, some later marginal Persian scribblings; acquired 1901 from Hall collection as a gift through Moore and Taylor.[5]

[1] The old Andover bookplate bears the marks A-4954 and ZE 607-1198 and the date Jan. 8, 1941. This is the MS described in Hatch's *Album,* plate 168.

[2] The number 10 has been added in the margin — but the writing is the same. The notation for Sel is faded, but not suspect. The detailed colophon equated 595 A.H., and Hatch reckoned the date as December 20, 1198.

[3] Vocalization diminishes as the volume goes on. This type of Estrangelo plus Nestorian contemporary vocalization is not that common. Cf. UTS MS Syr 1.

[4] One leaf loose.

115

[5] The wording on fly-leaves, or papers stuck into the volumes, suggests that Professors Moore and Taylor were aware of Hall's collection being available and arranged for someone to buy the manuscripts as a gift to the library.

AH MS 326 [formerly: AH Syr 2; And access 49614;[1] Cl 176]

THE NEW TESTAMENT IN THE PESHITTA RECENSION; 2053 Sel in Darband; Nestorian; occasional vocal; 2 col; 284 fol; 32 × 21 cm; paper; complete.

Details: Matthew 1*b;* Mark 37*b;* Luke 70*a;* John 102*a;* Acts 134*a;* James 177*b;* Philemon 268*a;*[2] gift of Taylor.

[1] The old Andover bookplate bears the marks A-4982; ZE 607 B471, dated June 7, 1898. On the binding one finds also an old marking Z110.
[2] The leaf containing the beginning of Hebrews is missing (or misplaced).

AH MS 327 [formerly: AH Syr 3; And access 50744; Cl 177]

THE STORY OF MAR YAHB-ALAHA AND RABBAN ṢAUMA; 1885(?) in Targawa; Nestorian; vocal; 84 fol; 22 × 17 cm; paper; complete.[1]

[1] From various notations in the volume it can be seen that the volume belonged to Benjamin Labaree, one of the early missionaries in Urmi. Afterwards it was part of Hall's collection from which it was purchased (1900). Hall dealt with this story *Proceedings AOS,* Oct. 1886 CXXVI — and I assume this is the one mentioned by Baumstark, *GSL* p. 326, n. 1. The curious note of Clemons can be traced to Hall's remark that the *Vorlage* of the manuscript was kept at that time (1886) at the seat of the patriarch in Kochannis.

116

AH MS 328   [formerly: AH Syr 4; And access 50745; Old shelf: safe 946; Cl 178][1]

THE STORY OF THE MARTYRDOM OF SHEM'ON BAR SABBA'Ē AND HIS COMPANIONS[2] AND A SHORT *VITA* OF APHREM; 1890 C.E. in Gawgtapah; Nestorian; vocal; 19 fol; (European pagination); 30 × 20 cm; paper; complete.

Details: Short *vita* of Aphrem in modern Syriac, p. 31.

[1]   This volume, like the preceding and the following ones, shares the fate of many Harvard codices: they were copied between 1880 and 1900, they reached a collector (Hall, Harris), they came to the library from his collection. This one was written in 1890 and came via Hall's collection to Andover in 1900.

[2]   Because of the *incipit* I had a quick look at Bedjan, *Acta Martyrum et Sanctorum* II (1891) 13f. The text seems identical. But the beginning in our manuscript raises linguistic suspicions: ܐܠ ܘܣ ܐܪ ....ܗܖܠ. I am not aware of a study on such "free scribal variations" which over-accentuate a syntactic phenomenon to a point which may be outside the limits of "classical" Syriac. Bedjan's text, of course, does not add *lan*. The present text needs further investigation.

AH MS 329   [formerly: AH Syr 5; And access 51950–53][1]

THE HEXAEMERON HOMILIES OF EMANUEL BAR SHAHARE; 1890 C.E.; in Gawgtapah; Nestorian (different hands); partly vocal; 211 fol;[2] 36 × 23 cm; paper; complete; cf. MS Syr 56.

Details: Contains homilies 3–28[3] and index; a homily by Chamīs Bar Ḳardaḥe is added and counted as No. 29; acquired in 1901 through Moore from Hall collection.

[1]   This information makes little sense. From looking at some old filing-cards I suspect that the following happened: the first Syriac MS of the library was given the number 51948, now AH MS 331. At that time it simply was counted with the Greek MSS. Then 51949 was acquired and then a lot of four MSS which were numbered 51950–53. Through some recent misinterpretation the entire se-

117

quence 51950–53 was interpreted to refer to this particular MS, and it was so marked. The accession number 51950 is that of MS 325.
[2] The main manuscript goes as far as p. 396, up to the beginning of Homily 27. Another MS of 13 fol has been added which starts with Homily 27 and continues to the end.
[3] Since Homily 2 is missing in most MSS, it would seem that our MS was copied from a *Vorlage* which lacked also Homily 1, as well as the end.

AH MS 330   [formerly: AH Syr 6; And access 51949]

A GRAMMAR OF SYRIAC, WRITTEN IN GARSHUNI;[1] ca 18 cent; Serto; partly vocal; 132 fol; 15 × 10 cm; Oriental leather and cardboard binding.[2]

[1] The headings are partly duplicated — Syriac and Garshuni.
[2] Some empty leaves have been scribbled upon in Garshuni and Arabic. This volume had belonged to Dr. Scott Watson, but it too seems to have come to AH via Hall's collection.

AH MS 331   [formerly: safe 763 Greek; And access 51948]

NESTORIAN MARRIAGE RITUAL;[1] Kanun II 2198 Sel; Nestorian; vocal; 60 (+2) fol; 18 × 11 cm; Oriental wood binding.

[1] The colophon title (European p. 118) is given as ܪܠܠܩܐܗ ܟܐܗܐ ܟܝܐܩܒ ܐܗ ܪܕܠܠܐܗܐ ܟܐܗܘܗ which seems to indicate that this is an "unabridged version." P. 19 starts the unit ܟܐܗܘܗ ܟܐܝܩܒ ܐ ܟܐܗܐ.

APPENDIX II

SYRIAC MANUSCRIPTS IN THE
UNION THEOLOGICAL SEMINARY, NEW YORK

A fair number of the Syriac items mentioned in American learned journals in the late 19th century are kept at the Union Theological Seminary (UTS) in New York. For some reason it would have appeared that some are Harvard items, the more so since most were described by Hall.[1] This appendix, then, should clarify the situation.[2]

In sheer numbers UTS may compete with Princeton Theological Seminary for the place of the second largest collection of Syriac manuscripts in America — very much behind Harvard. Yet only about two dozen items are proper MSS; the rest are odd leaves, partly remnants from bindings, etc. Most of the MSS are in bad shape, damaged, torn, with leaves missing. One wonders whether that was the reason why they were given to some of the missionaries. However, the collection also possesses a few good ancient codices.

I have looked at the UTS material in order to find out for myself certain facts pertaining to the Harvard collection. Altogether, I spent a few days in 1969 and in 1977[3], and this is no more than a check list.[4] As opposed to the Harvard collection which was never publicly described, UTS holdings were repeatedly listed in the last century.[5] The present arrangement is completely different[6] and old numbers have been mentioned where available. I need not add that this check list is less detailed than the preceding ones and the descriptions are summary, indeed.[7]

---

[1] As a rule, it seems that Hall described certain items which at the time already belonged to UTS, whereas items belonging to himself went largely to the two Harvard collections. I assumed at one stage of my work that because of Hall's connection with the Metropolitan Museum, at least some part of his collection would have gone there. I

119

do not think that any of the fragments now kept at the Metropolitan belonged to him. Cf. note on UTS MS Syr 5.

[2] As regards UTS, Clemons had little to fall back upon and the facts cannot be seen from his list.

[3] I am grateful to Dr. Robert Maloy, the present director, and to Mr. Richard K. Pachella, the former keeper of MSS and rare books, for their cooperation in my effort to arrange the collection and to look it over.

[4] The numbers of Clemons p. 495 have been mentioned where relevant. Only MSS 1, 2 and 5 had old "Cage" shelfmarks and only these were listed in the general catalogue of manuscripts at UTS.

[5] Many MSS contain old numbers which refer either to a list by Gottheil or a list by Hall, each of whom numbered differently. The list published in *JBL* 1885: 93f. seems to be based on preliminary information supplied by James Rogers, before the MSS actually came to America. Gottheil repeatedly studied the MSS and seems to have arranged them in collaboration with W.W. Rockwell, then librarian at UTS. But I have not seen a proper list by him.

[6] Cf. note on MS 31.

[7] I could not invest more time in clearing up certain points on which my notes were unclear. Thus, e.g., my notes for items 9, 12, 21 seem to indicate p. not f. This may be purely accidental — but, on the other hand, it may have been intentional, so that my final fol. notation is wrong.

UTS MS Syr 1   [Cage CB 42.7 n.d.; Cl 293]

THE NEW TESTAMENT IN THE PESHITTA RECENSION;[1] 10–11 cent;[2] Estrangelo; partly contemporary Nestorian vocal; 174 fol; 22 × 17 cm; wavy vellum; incomplete.

[1] The old label outside reads: Syriac New Testament found among the Nestorians. On the fly-leaf one finds: to Prof. N.W. Fiske from his brother in Christ Justin Perkins. From another note one learns that the volume came to UTS through Dr. James B. Gregg shortly before 1885.

[2] I cannot find any mention of the date 1180, as given by Clemons. I suspect that it comes from *JBL* 1885: 94. Hall wrote his report on the UTS manuscript on the basis of a preliminary announcement by Rogers, as mentioned above. I suspect Hall did not see the MS and

120

was misled. Hall referred at the time to the fact that a similar MS had been deposited in the "Congregational Library" in Boston thanks to Perkins. This may refer to MS Syr 4 of our catalogue although I cannot be sure. Cf. also AH MS 325.

UTS MS Syr 2   [Cage CB 42.7 11-; Cl 294]

THE NEW TESTAMENT IN THE PESHITTA RECENSION;[1] 12–13 cent; cursive Estrangelo; occasional vocal; 2 col; 146 fol; 18 × 13 cm; vellum; incomplete.[2]

[1] The MS contains Matthew 21:10–James 2:26. In his discussion Hall assumed (*JBL* 1883: 142f) that the MS contained originally the Gospels and the Catholic Epistles in 19 quires. As it stands, almost the entire volume is taken up by the Gospels. Many pages are faded and it is now interleaved.
[2] The volume was acquired by A.N. Andrus in Mardin and sent to Prof. Shudd at UTS in 1872. This is one of the well known Syriac Bibles because it came to a public library a century ago. The discussion in John Wright, *Historic Bibles in America* (1905) 123 does not contain first hand information.

UTS MS Syr 3

BOOK OF PRAYERS AND SERVICES;[1] 12–13 cent; cursive Estrangelo; 2 col; 96 fol; 43 × 34 cm; vellum; incomplete.

[1] This rather impressive volume seems to be for daily choral services and includes many *ba'utha's* attributed to Aphrem.

UTS MS Syr 4

GOSPEL LECTIONARY IN THE PESHITTA RECENSION; 16–17 cent; Nestorian;[1] partly vocal; 2 col; 95 fol; 26 × 18 cm; paper; incomplete.

[1] The script is somehow similar to MS Syr 135. Some headings are in Arabic.

UTS MS Syr 5   [Cage UK 6.3]

MARONITE BOOK OF PRAYERS AND SERVICES FOR SUNDAYS;[1] ca 18 cent; inelegant Serto (different hands); 215 fol; 9 × 7 cm; paper, incomplete.

[1] The outside label identified: *Maronite Church — Officium feriale Syrorum* and added the number 1835o. There is a note which reads: presented in 1898 by David H. McAlpin in the Isaac H. Hall collection of Greek Testaments. This would predate by two to three years acquisitions from Hall in Harvard.

UTS MS Syr 6[1]

NESTORIAN BOOK OF PRAYERS AND SERVICES;[2] Tamuz 1969 Sel; Nestorian; partly vocal; 198 fol; 28 × 21 cm; paper; complete.[3]

[1] This was once listed as MS No. 15.
[2] I am not sure whether *kaškol* and ܟܬܒܐ ܕܚܘܕܪܐ are interchangeable; both terms appear in the colophon. The rite is said to be according to the "upper convent."
[3] As remarked above, also "complete" codices can have loose and missing leaves.

UTS MS Syr 7[1]

NESTORIAN BOOK OF PRAYERS AND SERVICES; 18 cent; Nestorian; vocal; 2 col; 437 fol; 32 × 22 cm; paper; incomplete (fragmentary and loose); Oriental wooden binding.

[1] Cl 299 might possibly refer to this item. My notes of identifying *incipits* for offices are not good enough to state whether Macomber, "A list of the known manuscripts of the Chaldean Hudra," *OCP* 36 (1970) 129 No. 34 refers to this MS or to one of the neighboring items.

UTS MS Syr 8

NESTORIAN BOOK OF PRAYERS AND SERVICES; 18 cent; Nestorian (different hands); vocal; 380 fol; 32 × 21 cm; paper; incomplete (loose in binding).

UTS MS Syr 9[1]

NESTORIAN BOOK OF PRAYERS AND SERVICES; Nisan 2104 Sel; Nestorian; vocal; 284 fol; 22 × 16 cm; incomplete.[2]

[1] This was once listed as MS No. 3.
[2] Many leaves loose or lost; but long colophon on rite.

UTS MS Syr 10 [Cl 298]

NESTORIAN FUNERAL SERVICES;[1] Ab 2046 Sel in Darband; Nestorian; vocal; 138 fol; 23 × 16 cm; paper; complete (damaged and loose leaves).

[1] Once counted as MS No. 4. Hall printed a sample in *Hebraica* 4 (1888) 2f. and used the term "Service of Obsequies." The colophon term is ܥܝܢ ܠܕܬ ܟܘܣܬܐܕ ܟܬܠܝ. Cf. also *Proceedings AOS* 1889: CCXXX f. Hall counted 148 fol.

UTS MS Syr 11

'ABD-ĪŠŌ' BAR BERĪKHĀ: PARADISE OF EDEN; Iyar 2026 Sel; Nestorian; vocal; 104 fol; 32 × 22 cm; paper; complete.[1]

[1] A note in the end states: James E. Roger bought of Rabi Abraham Djala.

UTS MS Syr 12[1]

A VOLUME OF NESTORIAN THEOLOGICAL WRITINGS: THE "PEARL"[2] AND THE "BEE";[3] Tamuz 2007 Sel; Nestorian; 324 p; 21 × 15 cm; paper; complete.

[1] This was once listed as MS No. 16. It was once at Amherst College.

[2] I have not checked whether the copying together of Bar Berīkhā's *Pearl* and Solomon of Basra's *Bee* was common in other MSS. The *Bee* starts fol 82.

[3] Hall must have started work on this volume. But in *JBL* 6 (1886) 105 he knew that meanwhile the *Bee* had been edited by Budge.

UTS MS Syr 13

LITURGICAL PSALTER;[1] Adar 2096 Sel in Targawar; Nestorian; partly vocal; 2 col; 114 fol (in pages); 33 × 23 cm; paper; complete (parts missing); Oriental wood and leather binding.[2]

[1] This volume is characterized in the colophon as ܟܬܒܐ ܕܡܙܡܘ̈ܪܐ ܕܕܘܝܕ ܡܠܟܐ ܘܢܒܝܐ ܥܡ ܗܘܦܟܐ ܕܟܠܗ whereas the heading refers to ܐܬܟܬܒ ܗܢܐ ܟܬܒܐ ܕܝܠܗ ܕܡܫܡܫܢܐ. There are quite a number of marginal notes.

[2] Purchased by J.H. Shedd in 1885. I cannot make out why I jotted down at one time: apparently through Mingana and Gottheil. While some numberings of UTS go back to a list by Gottheil (see above), I do not recollect how Mingana might have got into my notes.

UTS MS Syr 14[1]

BOOK OF SERVICES AND PRAYERS;[2] Tamuz 2134 Sel; Nestorian; vocal; 160 fol; 17 × 11 cm; paper; complete.

[1] This was No. 14 in Gottheil's and No. 12 in Roger's listing. I take this to be Cl 306.

[2] Cf. UTS MS Syr 5. My knowledge does not go so far as to comprehend why a volume entitled ܟܬܒܐ ܕܬܫܡܫܬܐ ܕܥܕܬܐ ܕܡܪܘܢܝܐ is written in Nestorian characters. Also, I do not know whether ܡܪܘܢܝܐ would be a proper Maronite term. The colophon speaks of ܟܬܒܐ ܕܐܝܠܝܢ ܕܥܒܕܝ ܨܒܝܢܐ ܕܐܠܗܐ.

UTS MS Syr 15 [Cl 308][1]

GOSPEL LECTIONARY IN MODERN SYRIAC;[2] 1885 C.E.; Nestorian; 120 fol (ruled paginated European paper); 22 × 18 cm; paper; complete.[3]

[1] Former listings apparently Nos. 11 and 14.

[2] The translation is ascribed to a certain ܪܘܪܐܢܠܪ ܠܬܩ ܪܝܪܬܝܢ and a glance at the text makes one assume that it is some kind of "Proto-Alkosh" which should be investigated. From the explanation that Hall got concerning the MS it would look as if there was already an 18 cent dialectal *Vorlage*, i.e., that a dialectal Gospel Lectionary for Sundays according to the rite of the "upper convent" already existed about two centuries ago. This needs further study. Cf. MS Syr 147.

[3] This is one of the MSS which mentions the scribe. There is reason to assume that many of the new copies prepared for Rogers were penned by the same scribe, Ruel Ghoulphashon.

UTS MS Syr 16[1]

A VOLUME OF THEOLOGICAL WRITINGS, CONTAINING *VITAE* OF PROPHETS[2], THE CAVE OF TREASURES AND THE NICENE CREED; 19 cent; Nestorian; 150 fol; 23 × 19 cm; paper; complete.[3]

[1] It stands to reason that Clemons misread Hall's information. In any event, this is *one* volume — corresponding to Clemons 295–297. For the compositions, cf. perhaps MS Syr Kerkuk 9, Semences 38.

[2] Starting with the wonderdeeds of Epiphanius (of Cyprus). Cf. now the remarks of Ebied, *OCA* 1974: 523.

[3] This looks like MS 15 and must have been written at the same time. The writing is on paginated European ruled paper, written on *verso* only. The different items have been separated into different envelopes. The *Cave* starts fol 24 and the *Creed* fol 147. Cf. Hall, *JBL* 5 (1887) 28f.

UTS MS Syr 17

ISHO'DAD OF MERV: COMMENTARY ON THE GOSPELS; 18–19 cent;[1] Nestorian; vocal; 155 fol; 32 × 21 cm; paper; complete.[2]

[1] The colophon mentions 2000 Sel — there is some erasure. This may be the date of the Vorlage — this MS was not written in 1689.
[2] The MS got to UTS through Henry Preserved Smith.

UTS MS Syr 18[1]

THE GOSPEL OF MATTHEW IN MODERN SYRIAC;[2] 19 cent; Nestorian; vocal; 96 fol;[3] 36 × 22 cm; paper; incomplete.

[1] This was once listed as MS No. 13.
[2] The volume includes almost the whole of Matthew up to chapter 28. It came from J. Perkins and was presented by Rev. Hoadley in 1888.
[3] Pagination 6–198.

UTS MS Syr 19 [Cl 303]

LEXICOGRAPHICAL *OPUSCULES;*[1] 19 cent; Nestorian; vocal; 59 fol; 22 × 17 cm; paper; complete.

[1] I have chosen the title to be reminiscent of Hoffman's *Opuscula Nestoriana*. The resemblance was already stressed in Hall's original listing. The contents of this volume has been discussed in a lecture by Gottheil, *JAOS* 13 (1889) clxxxiv f. The heading is ܟܬܒܐ ܕܫܡܗܐ ܕܡܪܢ ܐܘܦܢܠܐ and may refer to both treatises. P. 71 the first treatise is referred to as ܟܬܒܐ ܕܗܘ ܫܘܠܡܐ ܟܠ ܗܘܦܟܐ ܕܗܘ ܣܘܢ. The second treatise, entitled ܗܛܘܟܣܐ ܕܥܒܝܕܐ ܠܐܝܢܐ ܕܗܘܩܢܐ ܕܦܛܗ ܟܬܒܐ ܕܗܘ ܒܝܬ ܓܙܐ (in rhymes), is ascribed to 'Abd-Īšō' of Gazarta.

126

UTS MS Syr 20 [Cl 301]

COMMEMORATIVE LIFE STORY OF RABBAN HORMIZD THE
PERSIAN;[1] 2006 Sel; Nestorian; vocal; 67 fol; 30 × 21 cm;
paper; complete; cf. MS Syr 67; 145.

[1] This particular MS was arranged for use in the Alqosh monastery
named after him. I have not studied the connection between the
"homily" and the monastery or monasteries.

UTS MS Syr 21 [Cl 304][1]

MAR BABAI: BOOK OF THE UNION; 1884 C.E.; Nestorian; partly
vocal; 2 col; 183 p; 36 × 22 cm; paper; complete.

[1] This seems to have been No. 20 in Gottheil's listing. In his article
Proceedings AOS 13(1889) cxl he dealt with the copyist — Osha'na of
Urmia.

UTS MS Syr 22

THE GOSPEL OF JOHN IN MODERN SYRIAC;[1] 1877 C.E.; Serto;
vocal; 67 fol (European ruled paper); 20 × 12 cm; incomplete.

[1] In contrast to most dialectal volumes in these collections, this one
is in the dialect of Tur Abdin. It includes the whole of John starting
with 6:25. The pages extant are 23–89. The volume came from the
collection of Henry Preserved Smith and is labelled on the outside:
unidentified dialect of Modern Syriac. This MS was once listed as MS
No. 27.

127

UTS MS Syr 23 [Cl 307]

QUESTIONS OF EZRA THE SCRIBE CONCERNING THE *ESCHATA;* [1]
19 cent; Nestorian; vocal; 10 fol;[2] 22 × 19 cm; paper.

[1] Hall dealt with this text in *Presbyterian Review* 7(1886) 537f.
Gottheil listed it as No. 16.
[2] European ruled paper written upon *recto* only.

UTS MS Syr 24

FRAGMENTS FROM A LECTIONARY OF THE EPISTLES;[1] ca 16 cent;
Nestorian; vocal; 4 fol; 21 × 15 cm; paper.

[1] These loose leaves from a binding may have belonged to
something similar to an *Apostolos,* but the material is not sufficient.
They were once listed as No. 11.

UTS MS Syr 25

FRAGMENT OF A HOMILY;[1] 19 cent; Nestorian; vocal; 20 fol; 22
× 18 cm; paper; incomplete.

[1] In this case the *explicit* might be useful for identification:
ܪܚܝܫܝܩܕܝ ܪܫܩܠ ܂ ܢܘܡܠܐ ܂ ܪܡܝ ܡܝ ܠܩܛܠ ܍ / ܪ ܂ ܝ ܂ ܪ ܂ ܝ ܪܚ ܂ ܕ ܂ ܩ ܂ ܕ ܂ ܝ ܂ ܢ ܂ ܝ ܂ ܡ ܂ ܝ ܂ ܂ ܂ ܪ ܂ ܠ ܂ ܪ ܂
ܪܨܠ ܂ ܝܡ ܂ ܢܘܡܠܐ ܂ ܡ ܂ ܪ ܂ ܠ ܂ / ܪ ܂ ܕ ܂ ܚ ܂ ܪ ܂ ܪ ܂ ܬ ܂ ܪ ܂ ܠ ܂ ܪ ܂ ܪ ܂ ܝ ܂ ܡ ܂ ܝ ܂ ܪ ܂ ܬ ܂ ܪ ܂ ܠ ܂ ܘ ܂ /
ܪ ܂ ܝ ܂ ܪ ܂ ܕ ܂ ܪ ܂ ܝ. This MS was once listed as No. 23.

UTS MS Syr 26

FRAGMENT FROM A NESTORIAN BOOK OF PRAYERS;[1] 18 cent;
Nestorian; 1 fol; 15 × 14 cm; paper.

[1] Most of the following fragments consist of one leaf, usually torn
or cut, partly illegible. All paper.

128

UTS MS Syr 27

FRAGMENT OF EXEGETICAL LEXICON ON NEW TESTAMENT;[1] 18 cent; Nestorian; partly vocal; 1 fol; 16 × 11 cm; paper.

[1] The fragmentary leaf may have served as a bookmark. It was once listed as No. 20, then as No. 48.

UTS MS Syr 28

FRAGMENT FROM NESTORIAN BOOK OF PRAYERS;[1] 18 cent; Nestorian; partly vocal; 1 fol; 14 × 11 cm.

[1] This item was once listed as No. 25.

UTS MS Syr 29[1]

FRAGMENT FROM NESTORIAN BOOK OF PRAYERS; 18 cent; Nestorian; occasional vocal; 4 fol; 20 × 14 cm.

[1] This item was once listed as No. 26.

UTS MS Syr 30

FRAGMENT OF GOSPEL LECTIONARY IN THE PESHITTA RECENSION;[1] 17–18 cent; inelegant Nestorian Estrangelo; partly vocal; 2 fol; 27 × 19 cm; paper.

[1] Contains parts of Mark XVI; John IV; XIV–XVI. It was once listed as No. 15 and then as No. 30.

UTS MS Syr 31

PASSION STORY OF ST. GEORGE;[1] 18 cent; inelegant Nestorian; partly vocal; 19 fol; 18 × 11 cm; incomplete.

[1] This item was once listed as No. 31. All subsequent MSS have been arranged according to their numbering in some previous listing.

UTS MS Syr 32 [Cl 305]

PARTS OF THE HISTORY OF THE VIRGIN; 18 cent;[1] inelegant Nestorian; partly vocal; 64 p; 22 × 16 cm; incomplete and pages out of sequence.

[1] I do not think this is identical with the MS listed originally by Hall as No. 11, and thus identified as Cl 305. The present item came from Gottheil in 1935. Gottheil noted in this copy pages of Budge's edition.

UTS MS Syr 33

FRAGMENT OF ZOZIMUS CONCERNING THE RECHABITES;[1] Elul 2000 Sel; Nestorian; vocal; 36 p;[2] 22 × 16 cm; incomplete.

[1] For the known MSS of this text cf. Baumstark, *GSL* p. 251, n. 5. Also this MS belonged to Gottheil and was presented in 1935. Cf. Nau, *RS* VI–VII. The volume could be described as consisting of two parts, since p. 27 starts a series of prayers for various occasions (e.g., blessing of the cup; prayer for the grain).
[2] The MS contained originally ca 100 p.

UTS MS Syr 34 [Cl 311]

FIRST AND SECOND LETTERS FROM HEAVEN;[1] 18 cent; Nestorian; vocal; 42 p; 16 × 12 cm; complete.

[1] The first leaf contains some prayers.

UTS MS Syr 35

PRAYER FOR THE HEALTH OF THE BISHOP AND THE GOOD OF THE COMMUNITY; ca 1800; Nestorian; 1 fol, fragmentary and cut; presented by Gottheil.

UTS MS Syr 36

DAMAGED FRAGMENT FROM MARTYR STORY; ca 1800; inelegant Nestorian; 7 × 5 cm.

UTS MS Syr 37

DAMAGED FRAGMENT OF DIALOGUE OF PRAISE BY CHERUBS, ETC.; 18 cent; Nestorian; partly vocal; 1 fol; 16 × 12 cm.

UTS MS Syr 38

FRAGMENT OF HOMILY ON NATURE OF JESUS; 18 cent; Nestorian; 1 fol (one side only); 15 × 12 cm.

UTS MS Syr 39

FRAGMENT OF NESTORIAN BOOK OF PRAYERS;[1] ca 1800; cursive Nestorian-Estrangelo; occasional vocal; 1 fol; 26 × 15 cm.

[1] It appears that this is the fragment mentioned by Macomber, *OCP* 36 (1970) 120f.

UTS MS Syr 40

PRAYER FOR THE HEALTH OF THE BISHOP AND THE GOOD OF THE COMMUNITY;[1] ca 1800; Nestorian; vocal; 1 fol; 19 × 15 cm.

[1] The contents are similar to that of MS 35.

131

UTS MS Syr 41

FRAGMENT OF MARTYR'S STORY IN METRE;[1] ca 1800; inelegant Nestorian; 1 fol; 15 × 8 cm.

[1] It would seem this was actually part of a prayer book, but the material is too meager.

UTS MS Syr 42

FRAGMENT FROM A TREATISE OF THEOLOGICAL QUERIES;[1] ca 1800; inelegant Nestorian; 1 fol; 16 × 10 cm.

[1] Among the portions that can be deciphered is one on the change of the nature of Lot's wife and one on the wood of the cross.

UTS MS Syr 43

FRAGMENT OF STORY ON TROUBLES IN A COMMUNITY;[1] ca 1800; inelegant Nestorian; occasional vocal; 1 fol; 15 × 10 cm.

[1] One side of the leaf contains the end of a story about someone, ending with a curse; then continuing about some troubles in the community. The other side seems a scribal exercise. The language is influenced by Modern Syriac.

UTS MS Syr 44

SCRIBAL EXERCISE;[1] Nestorian; 34 × 23 cm.

[1] This is an exercise on a piece of carton by the wife of one of the early missionaries, Mrs. Judith Grant, who tried her hand in writing "with a reed, after the manner of the Nestorians."

132

UTS MS Syr 45

DAMAGED FADED FRAGMENT OF NESTORIAN BOOK OF PRAYERS;
ca 1800; 1 fol (from binding); 9 × 7 cm.

UTS MS Syr 46

COLOPHON AS SCRIBAL EXERCISE; ca 1800; Nestorian; 1 fol; 15
× 13 cm.

UTS MS Syr 47

SCRIBAL EXERCISE; 19 cent; Nestorian; 3 fol;[1] 37 × 23 cm.

[1] The item consists of one double and one regular fol. The exercise
exists in copying out on one side a sentence from the Lord's Prayer
in modern Syriac and on the other side a didactic poem in classical
Syriac. A note explained that this was written for D.T. Stoddard. The
writing, however, looks non-professional, rather as if written by one
of the missionaries. I did not indulge in comparing the hand to that
of Stoddard's autographs, kept at Yale. Also this item came to UTS
thanks to Henry Preserved Smith.

UTS MS Syr 48

DAMAGED FRAGMENT OF PHARMACEUTICAL OR MAGICAL
PRESCRIPTION;[1] ca 1800; Nestorian; 25 × 10 cm.

[1] The fragment is stuck to a wooden binding. It may have come
there as part of a binding.

GENERAL INDEX

(Numbers refer to manuscripts)

134

138

PLATES

By permission of the Semitic Museum
and the Houghton Library, Harvard University

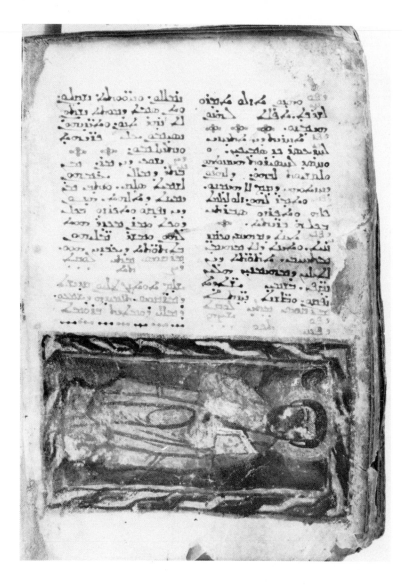

PLATE I: MS Syr 2 fol 63

144

PLATE II: MS Syr 20

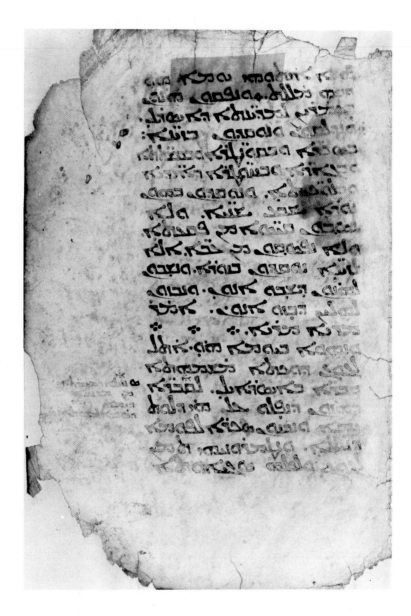

PLATE III: MS Syr 28

146

PLATE IV: MS Syr 63 fol 5

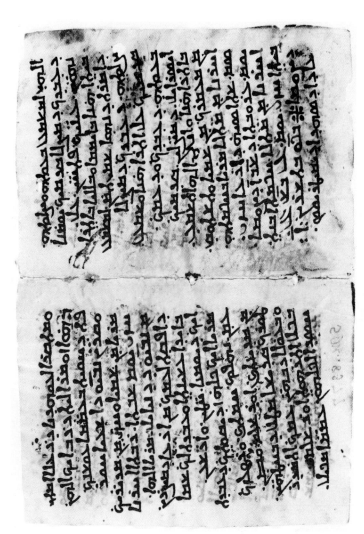

148

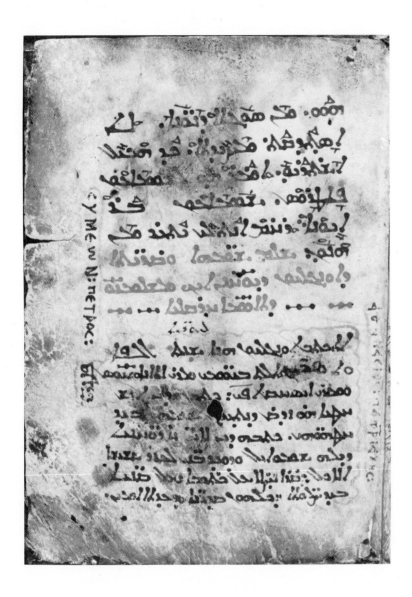

PLATE VI: MS Syr 176 colophon

149